Girls and Exclusion

The widespread view that girls are succeeding in education and are therefore 'not a problem' is a myth. By drawing directly on girls' own accounts and experiences of school life and those of professionals working with disaffected youth, this book offers startling new perspectives on the issue of exclusion and underachievement amongst girls.

The book demonstrates how the social and educational needs of girls and young women have slipped down the policy agenda in the UK and internationally. The authors argue for a re-definition of school exclusion which covers the types of exclusion commonly experienced by girls, such as truancy, self-exclusion, or school drop-out as a result of pregnancy. Drawing on girls' own ideas, the authors make recommendations as to how schools might develop as more inclusive communities where the needs of both boys and girls are addressed equally.

This book is essential reading for postgraduate students, teachers, policy-makers and LEA staff dedicated to genuine social and educational inclusion.

Audrey Osler is Professor of Education and Director of the Centre for Citizenship Studies in Education at the University of Leicester.

Kerry Vincent was employed as a Research Fellow at the Centre for Citizenship Studies in Education before taking the position of Educational Psychologist with Cheshire LEA.

D0813418

Girls and Exclusion

Rethinking the agenda

Audrey Osler and Kerry Vincent

RoutledgeFalmer
Taylor & Francis Group

LONDON AND NEW YORK

First published 2003 by RoutledgeFalmer
11 New Fetter Lane, London EC4P 4EE

Simultaneously published in the USA and Canada
by RoutledgeFalmer
29 West 35th Street, New York, NY 10001

RoutledgeFalmer is an imprint of the Taylor & Francis Group

© 2003 Audrey Osler and Kerry Vincent

Typeset in Goudy by RefineCatch Limited, Bungay, Suffolk
Printed and bound in Great Britain by
TJ International Ltd, Padstow, Cornwall

British Library Cataloguing in Publication Data
A catalogue record for this book is available from the British Library

Library of Congress Cataloging in Publication Data
Osler, Audrey.
    Girls and exclusion : rethinking the agenda / Audrey Osler and
Kerry Vincent.
        p.   cm.
    Includes bibliographical references and index.
    ISBN 0–415–30315–X – ISBN 0–415–30316–8 (pbk.)
    1. Student suspension – Great Britain.   2. Student expulsion –
Great Britain.   3. Girls – Education – Great Britain.   I. Vincent,
Kerry, 1961– .   II. Title.
  LB3089.4.G7 O84 2003
  371.5′43 – dc21   2002036707

ISBN 0–415–30315–X (hbk)
ISBN 0–415–30316–8 (pbk)

Contents

Foreword

In contemporary Australia, New Zealand, England, Scotland, Northern Ireland, Scandinavia, Europe, Canada and the USA, popular and policy discussions about the relationships between gender and schooling are dominated by concerns about the education of boys (Hayes, 1998). Issues associated with girls' education have all but disappeared from public debate and policy (see, however, Social Exclusion Unit, 1999; Bullen, Kenway and Hey, 2000). Indeed, the debate is couched in such a way as to give the impression that no issues remain about girls' education. All girls are implicitly portrayed as winners and all boys as losers. Indeed, the insinuation is that girls' success has been at the expense of boys' failure. The situation is different in research circles. While articles and books about boys dominate the literature, only some treat boys as a unified group and implicitly blame females for boys' alleged failure (e.g. West, 1995; Biddulph, 1997). However, most such literature focuses on the differences between boys and the implications of such differences for their educational experiences and outcomes (e.g. Mac an Ghaill, 1996; Gilbert and Gilbert, 1998). Although articles on girls and more broadly on education and gender relations continue to be published, scholarly books on girls and schooling are relatively rare (see, however, Walkerdine, Lucey and Melody, 2001). For this reason alone this book is welcome but of course it is also welcome for important other reasons as I will go on to explain.

The concern about boys has led to numerous government inquiries and reports. In 1999 Cherry Collins, Julie McLeod and I were commissioned by the Australian government to undertake an overview and analysis of the existing databases and research findings in this country. We were required to identify and explain the ways in which gender is connected to school retention, participation, performance and post-school destinations. We were also asked to assess the relative impact of such other variables as geographical location, ethnicity and socio-economic status. The implicit aim in the latter case was to move the current public and policy debates about gender beyond the simplistic binary logic that had character-ised them to date. The aim was to move it beyond what we called the 'gender see-saw' approach to one that recognised complexity; we called it the 'gender jig saw' approach. Such recognition of complex-ity is evident in this book. Although its focus is on girls, it attends to what we have called elsewhere 'geometries of multiple differences' (Kraack and Kenway, 2002). This is a hybrid term that blends Hara-way's (1991) notion of a 'geometry of difference' and Massey's (1993) 'power-geometry'. As we argue:

> This concept allows the different vectors of identity (including class, gender, ethnicity, sexuality and age) to be considered within the dynamics of contemporary circumstances. Different strands of identity are examined as they move across time and space. The notion 'geometries of multiple differences' does not prioritize any one identity vector, but views each in relation to the others within constantly changing contexts.
>
> (Kraack and Kenway, 2002: 147)

Our report (Collins, Kenway and McLeod, 2000b) points to the many nuances and complexities of the connections between gender and education across time and space and in particular it clarifies 'which girls and which boys' can be understood as educationally disadvantaged. The Report demonstrates that girls and boys from backgrounds that are of 'low socio-economic status' (SES) are the most disadvantaged students. We argue that

> girls and boys from low SES groups tend to be disadvantaged in the following ways:
>
> - Many more of them face the risks associated with leaving school early.
> - Many more select school subjects, subject clusters and post school education and training that largely lead them towards low SES employment.
> - Many more of them have lower school achievement which severely restricts their educational and career choices and

thus increases the chance of their social exclusion and of cumulative social disadvantage.

(Collins, Kenway and McLeod, 2000b: 7–8)

Our report also suggests that their particular disadvantages may be manifest differently according to gender, race and locality and that more research needs to be conducted into such differences (Collins, Kenway and McLeod, 2000b: 7–8).

At the time of writing the report we were unable to locate any studies that looked at the question of school exclusion (or 'suspension and expulsion' as we call it in Australia), let alone any that considered girls and exclusion as this book does. The related focus then was on school retention – that is, on staying on at or leaving school. Indeed, many major government policies around the world have been directed towards ensuring that students stay at school for as long as possible and certainly beyond the compulsory years. Such policies in Australia include curriculum reform, vocational education in schools, and various youth and family allowances schemes. Remaining at school through Years 11 and 12 has thus become the norm and leaving early is considered a problem, particularly if students leave during or before Year 10 (under-age school leavers). As we demonstrated, there are links between gender and retention, but to best understand the links, a nuanced reading of the figures related to school and post-school life is required.

The data we considered showed that girls' rates of retention in Australia have steadily increased, and boys' rates have ebbed and flowed in accordance with ups and downs in the economy. Currently boys are leaving school earlier than girls and many read this as a further disadvantage experienced by boys in comparison with girls. However, we showed that leaving school early is not always problematic for all boys since boys who leave school early are better able to access work and training than are girls. But of course leaving early is particularly problematic for some boys who are more likely to be 'unemployed' than the girls who leave early. That said, it is vital to note that leaving school early is almost always problematic for girls. Girls find it far more difficult to access paid work than their male peers and they tend to be significantly over-represented in the 'out of the labour market' figures as we explain further in Collins, Kenway and McLeod (2000a). Under-age school leavers of both sexes face particular problems. Drawing on Australian data which are unfortunately not broken down by gender, Brooks *et al.* (1997)

estimate that those who leave school between the ages of 12 and 14 years could amount to 1–4 per cent of the total age group, that at least twice that number are at risk of becoming under-age school leavers; and that there are heavy concentrations of such students whose lives are characterised by poverty.

One of the many important contributions of this book is that it takes us behind the retention debate. It shows that leaving and staying are only the surface manifestations of a much more complicated story about presence, absence and schooling. It explains that there are many ways of being absent while actually at school and many manifestations of absence from school – official and unofficial, short and longer term, temporary and permanent, self- and other-imposed. The catch-all notion of exclusion, Osler and Vincent explain, does not capture these differences adequately, and their book shows that these different modalities of exclusion are strongly inflected by gender, race and social class. Of course, in England this matter has been canvassed to some degree. As the authors explain, policy attention has been paid to boys and exclusion. Indeed, exclusion from schooling in England is either seen as a problem for boys in general or a problem for particular groups of boys. Consequently, most of the practices that flow from this policy are designed with boys in mind, even though girls constitute quite a significant minority of those excluded.

Again, what we see here is a superficial reading of a complicated story and limited practices flowing from this restricted reading. Indeed, as Osler and Vincent point out, this reading is particularly unreflective about the connections between gender and exclusion. Not only does it fail to examine its own assumptions, it also fails to benefit from the insights produced by many feminist and 'critical masculinity' (see Whitehead and Barrett, 2001) scholars about the subtle connections between gender and schooling. Osler and Vincent remind us of the benefits of such insights as they unpack the available data, produce their own data and provide a reading that pays proper attention to the many subtleties involved. One such insight arrived at long ago but clearly 'forgotten' in the current ferment over 'boys behaving badly' is that notions of 'the good student' and 'the successful student', and their converse, tend to be very narrowly framed (see further, Kenway and Willis, with Blackmore and Rennie, 1998). Such framings usually fail to acknowledge the 'geometries of multiple differences' noted above. One implication of such framing is that certain boys' and certain girls' 'bad' behaviour can become 'hyper-visible' and can attract both positive and negative teacher attention. But equally such 'hyper-visibility' can hide from view other students who perform and/or behave badly but do so quietly and thus slip off teachers' radar screens. As Osler and Vincent indicate, this happens with many girls whose exclusion in its various forms goes unnoticed. Their exclusion becomes invisible because it does not fit the dominant view of exclusion. And, because it does not fit the dominant view and the corrective practices associated with such a view, it goes unremediated. This, among many examples, assists Osler and Vincent to make a compelling case for re-thinking matters of inclusion and exclusion.

Their case is compelling for many reasons and I do not need to repeat them here. But I do wish to point out the importance of the girls' eye view offered throughout the text. The dominant concern about the education of boys has been accompanied by many calls from boys' advocates for educators and policy-makers to 'listen to boys'. As a result, boys' views of what schools lack for them and how they might improve are now filtering into books about boys and into suggestions for educational reform (e.g. *Standing Committee of Education and Training*, 2002). This has of course meant there is little interest in listening to girls and in this the book is a refreshing change. The girls' stories about their experiences of schooling and the connections they draw between such experiences and their exclusion are very telling indeed. Their stories about the push–pull factors associated with exclusion give us all reason to pause; so too do their stories about their preferences for other forms of educational provision. Such stories build on much research evidence which shows that the learning environments typical of conventional schools often compound rather than address the problems of disaffected school students or those seeking to return to school. As we have argued with regard to Australia, indigenous youth, refugees and recent arrivals, rural and remote youth, young mothers, juvenile offenders, young people with learning difficulties and delays, young people with a range of disabilities, homeless young people and wards of the state are often poorly served by conventional schools (Collins, Kenway and McLeod, 2000b). Ours and other studies encourage schools to adopt the sorts of learning programmes and environments that have been shown to be compatible with such young people's success (e.g. Brooks *et al.*, 1997). Clearly, alternative modes of providing them with support must be further developed within and beyond schooling as we know it.

So, this book is particularly important given the widespread and clearly misplaced notion that schooling is now 'friendly' to all girls. And the book is important for other reasons too. Underlying many calls encouraging people to listen to boys are rather naïve notions of truth and communication. Implicit here is the view that boys speak the unmitigated facts about their circumstances and that listeners hear this truth in an unmediated manner. Clearly listening is always a process of translation and so too is speech. Both are situated, partial and interested. Boys' and girls' views about their schooling and its connections to gender and other axes of power will always contain elements of both blindness and insight. The danger of this emphasis on listening is that it may lead to policies and practices that build on the blindnesses rather than the insights and so re-inscribe traditional gender identities that are no longer viable in these times which require a certain gender fluidity and flexibility (Kenway and Kelly, 2000). While important, students' understanding of gender and schooling needs to be complemented by other standpoints. This book also offers the views of the various professionals involved and thus provides other layers of analysis that offer additional insights on the problems and issues. But it does not stop there. Unlike some of the policy documents on boys' education and some of the literature produced by boys' advocates, it reads these various narratives in association with the systematic and scholarly inquiry that already exists on gender and schooling and that has been built up over many years. In other words it also 'listens to' rather than ignores the research of others and seeks to build upon it. Further, it does not just offer a richly informed interpretation of the issues. It also points to some important ways in which circumstances must be otherwise for girls at school.

Given the invisibility of many of the exclusions associated with the girls under scrutiny here and given the pressing need for things to change, this book should mark a turning point in current debates about gender and schooling. It directs our attention to those girls whose schools serve them badly and to those practices that exclude them not only from school but also from many other economic and social benefits. It offers a sophisticated rendering of gender issues in schools today as they affect girls and invites policy-makers and practitioners to move past their focus on boys alone and to attend to the needs of those students in most difficulty.

References

Biddulph, S. (1997) *Raising Boys*, Lane Cove, Australia: Finch Publishing.

Brooks, M., Milne, C., Paterson, K., Johannson, K. and Hart, K. (1997) *Under-age School Leaving: a report to the National Youth Affairs Research Scheme*, Hobart: National Clearing House of Youth Studies.

Bullen, E., Kenway, J. and Hey, V. (2000) New Labour, social exclusion and educational risk management: the case of 'gymslip mums', *British Educational Research Journal*, 26 (4): 441–56.

Collins C., Kenway J. and McLeod J. (2000a) Gender debates we still have to have, *Australian Educational Researcher*, 27 (3): 37–48.

Collins, C., Kenway, J. and McLeod, J. (2000b) *Factors influencing educational performance of males and females in school and their initial destinations after leaving school*, Department of Education, Training and Youth Affairs, Canberra. http://www.detya.gov.au/schools/publications/index.htm

Gilbert, R. and Gilbert, P. (1998) *Masculinity Goes to School*, Sydney: Allen and Unwin.

Haraway, D. (1991) *Simians, Cyborgs and Women: the reinvention of nature*, London: Free Association Books.

Hayes, D. (1998) The displacement of girls as the 'educationally disadvantaged' subject: a genealogical tale, *Change: Transformations in Education* 1 (2): 7–15.

Kenway, J. and Kelly, P. (2000) Local global labour markets and the restructuring of gender schooling and work, in N. Stromquist and K. Monkman (eds), *Globalisation and Education: integration and contestation across cultures*, Lanham, MD: Rowman and Littlefield.

Kenway, J. and Willis, S. with Blackmore, J. and Rennie, L. (1998) *Answering Back: Girls, boys and feminism in schools*, London: Routledge.

Kraack, A. and Kenway J. (2002) 'Place, time and stigmatised youthful identities: bad boys in paradise', *Journal of Rural Sociology*, 18 (2): 145–55.

Mac an Ghaill, M. (1996) 'What about the boys?' Schooling class and crisis masculinity, *Sociological Review*, 44 (3), 381–97.

Massey, D. (1993) 'Power-Geometry' and a progressive sense of place, in J. Bird, B. Curtis, G. Robertson and L. Tricker (eds) *Mapping the Futures: local culture, global change*, London: Routledge.

Social Exclusion Unit (1999) *Teenage Pregnancy* (Cm4342) (Online, accessed 11 October 1999, URL: http://www.cabinet-office.gov.uk/seu/1999/teenpar/index.htm).

Standing Committee of Education and Training (2002), *Report of the Inquiry into the Education of Boys. Boys: getting it right*, http://www.aph.gov.au/house/committee/edt/Eofb/index.HTM

Walkerdine, V., Lucey, H. and Melody, J. (2001) *Growing Up Girl: psychosocial explorations of gender and class*, Basingstoke: Macmillan-Palgrave.

West, P. (1995) *Giving Boys a Ray of Hope: masculinity and education*, Sydney: Discussion Paper for the Gender Equity Taskforce, Australia.

Whitehead, S. and Barrett, F. (2001) *The Masculinities Reader*, Cambridge: Polity Press.

Jane Kenway
Division of Arts Education and Social Sciences
University of South Australia

Acknowledgements

We wish to thank a number of people who have supported us in the writing of this book.

In particular we acknowledge the young women who participated in the research project, for their insights and perceptions. We also are grateful to the parents and to the many professionals working with young people who generously gave us time to interview them or provided us with information.

Special thanks to Cathy Street of New Policy Institute who was co-director of the *Girls and School Exclusion* project. We appreciated working with you and learning from you in the course of the research and acknowledge the considerable contribution you have made in enabling us to write this book. We also wish to thank Marie Lall who was a researcher on the project and Peter Kenway of New Policy Institute for their substantial contributions.

We extend our thanks to the Joseph Rowntree Foundation for funding the research. We are particularly grateful to Susan Taylor for her input, support and enthusiasm throughout the study and to Dave Utting for helping to bring our work to the attention of policy-makers.

We appreciate the contributions of the advisory group which supported our original study: Mog Ball, Howard Firth, Margaret Holland, Julie O'Mahoney, Barbara Rayment, Terry Ryall, Darshan Sachdev, Joan Stead.

A number of other people have provided us with advice and information: Nicky Darlow, Helen Lindstrom, Clair Trainor.

We also acknowledge the substantial contributions of colleagues in the School of Education and the Centre for Citizenship Studies in Education at the University of Leicester. Barbara Hall and Samantha Keenan provided encouragement and much valued administrative support at different stages of the project. Hugh Starkey read the text and has also given us support, critical advice and much encouragement.

Acronyms and Abbreviations

ADHD	Attention Deficit Hyperactivity Disorder
BBC	British Broadcasting Corporation
CAMHS	Child and Adolescent Mental Health Services
CD	Conduct Disorder
CRC	Convention on the Rights of the Child
CRE	Commission for Racial Equality
DfEE	Department for Education and Employment (now DfES)
DfES	Department for Education and Skills
EBD	Emotional and Behavioural Difficulties
EWO	Education Welfare Officer
FE	Further Education
GCE A level	General Certificate of Education, Advanced Level
GCSE	General Certificate of Secondary Education
IEA	International Association for the Evaluation of Educational Achievement
LEA	Local Education Authority
NAHT	National Association of Headteachers
ODD	Oppositional Defiant Disorder
OFSTED	Office for Standards in Education
PLASC	Pupil Level Annual School Census
PRU	Pupil Referral Unit
SAP	Structural Adjustment Programme
SEG	Special Education Grant
SEN	Special Educational Needs
SEU	Social Exclusion Unit

Introduction
Rethinking exclusion and inclusion

At first glance, girls seem to have benefited most from developments in education over recent years. They appear to be outperforming boys in school-leaving examinations in a range of international contexts, and are now more likely than boys to enter higher education in many countries. Educators, politicians and journalists have all focused their attention on boys, who are commonly assumed to be underachieving. But concern about boys' 'underachievement' hides some real problems facing many girls and young women. The rhetoric about boys' 'failure' and girls' 'success' masks a reality where there are vast differences in educational experiences and opportunities among girls, as there are among boys.

Disparities between rhetoric and reality are most marked in relation to the issue of exclusion or expulsion from school, where most attention has focused on boys, who form the vast majority in the official exclusion figures. For example, in England, girls comprise one in four of those subject to formal, permanent disciplinary exclusion from secondary school. Official estimates suggest that 1,566 girls were excluded in this way in 2000/2001 (DfES, 2002). Although girls form a substantial minority of students subject to disciplinary exclusion, they have been largely overlooked in school exclusion prevention strategies and research.

Research conducted at school and local education authority (LEA) levels suggests that as schools have cut the number of permanent exclusions, in line with Government targets, the numbers of both temporary and unrecorded (unofficial) exclusions have risen (Osler *et al.*, 2000). Some young people experience a number of fixed-term exclusions before finally being excluded on a permanent basis. The official statistics therefore present only a fraction of the number of young people who may be out of school as a result of disciplinary action.

Very few girls are excluded from primary school and it is during adolescence that the number of exclusions rises sharply. Students of both sexes are most commonly permanently excluded at ages 13 and 14, in Years 9 and 10 of their school careers, at the point when preparation for key school-leaving examinations begins. A similar pattern can be found in New Zealand where the vast majority of students who are subject to suspension from school are aged 13–15 years (Alton-Lee and Praat, 2001).

In this book we draw on a range of research projects on exclusion from school, carried out between 1996 and 2001. We focus in particular on our research into girls and school exclusion in England carried out in 2000–2001 and funded by the Joseph Rowntree Foundation. The project was a joint venture between the Centre for Citizenship Studies in Education at the University of Leicester and the New Policy Institute (NPI) in London and was directed by Audrey Osler and Cathy Street. A short report of the research has been published (Osler et al., 2002).

A special feature of our research is that we draw on girls' own perceptions of school life and of the various forms of exclusion which operate. By interrogating girls' own accounts and those of a range of professionals working in education, health, social services and voluntary sector agencies, we are able to identify a complex picture of young women's needs. These professionals included service providers working with young people in alternative educational provision and other community settings (for example, teachers, social workers, health professionals, youth workers) who were also able to help us identify examples of effective services which were meeting girls' varied needs and to identify gaps in provision.

We explore the difficulties and potential causes of disaffection among secondary school-age girls, examining these in the context of unequal power relations in schools and in teachers' differentiated responses according to gender, class and ethnicity. We analyse specific responses of service providers to girls from a range of communities, in the light of the perspectives of the young women, their parents and professionals who work with them.

We consider how schools, local authorities and voluntary agencies allocate resources to address young people's needs and problems. We also examine how girls access the provision on offer. There is a widespread assumption that help is equally available to girls and to boys. Yet much of the help available is generated by overtly challenging behaviour, more commonly exhibited by boys, and by disciplinary exclusion. Those girls who deal with their problems in other ways and who do not attract attention to themselves are often judged by professionals as 'not a problem'. The responses of these young women when in difficulty can result in them not receiving help.

We identified a diverse range of strategies designed to promote school inclusion and longer-term social inclusion among the young. Current provision is largely dominated by boys. Not only do many girls feel unable to take up the help on offer, but many professionals do not refer girls, judging it to be inappropriate, given the gender imbalance. This results in further male over-representation and makes it even more unlikely that girls will access support.

Although girls form a minority among those students who experience formal, officially recorded, disciplinary exclusion, they are particularly vulnerable to other types of exclusion from school. Their behaviour patterns and their responses to difficulties also mean that their problems are often more difficult for professionals to detect than those of boys. Girls who encounter difficulties often drop out of school, truant or engage in other forms of self-exclusion. There is evidence to suggest that the amount of school being missed by some girls, as a result of unofficial exclusion, truancy, and caring responsibilities, is significantly underestimated.

We propose a re-definition of exclusion, as it applies to girls (see chapter 2), recognising that it can occur through systemic problems in schools, feelings of isolation, unresolved personal, family or emotional problems, bullying, withdrawal or truancy as well as being the result of formal disciplinary procedures. We argue that for many girls, informal and unrecognised exclusion is as significant as formal disciplinary exclusion. It can restrict or deny girls their right to education and lead to more general social exclusion. We further argue that unless policy-makers and service providers broaden their definition of exclusion from school to encompass girls' experiences it is unlikely that they will successfully address the longer-term policy goal of combating social exclusion.

Research design and methodology

Our in-depth, largely qualitative study was based in six sample areas: three local education authorities and three education action zones in

England.[1] Our aim was to identify the specific challenges and difficulties which some girls experience in school and which lead to disaffection or exclusion in some form. Our practical goals were to enhance understanding and awareness among service providers, policy-makers and researchers of girls' varied experiences and needs in secondary schools and to identify ways in which these needs can be addressed.

Our initial fieldwork took place from 2000 to 2001. We interviewed a total of 81 girls of secondary school age, in groups and individually. The sample included girls who were not causing concern in school, those who were judged by their teachers to be at risk of exclusion and some who had been excluded in the past. Ten parents (all mothers) whose daughters had experienced difficulties, including exclusion, were also interviewed. We wished to gain some insight into their perceptions of the support offered to their daughters.

We also analysed data from 55 interviews with service providers in each of the six areas. Interviewees included staff in mainstream schools, pupil referral units (PRUs), educational psychology and education welfare services, behavioural support teams and education facilities for schoolgirl mothers. Several youth workers and social services personnel were also interviewed.

A random selection of 20 further education colleges across England were contacted by telephone to establish provision for disaffected under-16 year-olds. Data from telephone interviews were supplemented by documents from these institutions. Additionally, we collected data from a range of education action zones and health action zones, units for pregnant schoolgirls and young mothers, and special projects for young people in difficulties or with specific needs.

Girls and Exclusion draws on data gathered from all six of the sample areas. It focuses particularly on three sample areas, with quotations from girls, their parents and service providers drawn from these three areas. These are an education action zone within a Midlands unitary authority, where poverty and unemployment are high; a large Midlands metropolitan LEA, which includes both prosperous and socially deprived areas; and a unitary authority in the South, which is generally prosperous, but with some pockets of deprivation. From the three sample areas 43 girls took part in group interviews and 29 were subsequently interviewed individually. Of the 43 girls, 11 were from minority ethnic communities. Of the 29 individual interviewees, 21 were white, and eight were drawn from African Caribbean, South Asian and mixed heritage backgrounds.

The majority of girls we interviewed in these three areas were being educated in mainstream schools (n34[2]), with six attending pupil referral units and three attending a further education college. Eight girls had experienced permanent exclusion; in most cases, the permanent exclusion had been proceeded by several fixed-term exclusions. A further five had received fixed-term exclusions only. Three of the 43 had experienced an 'internal exclusion', being excluded from certain lessons but remaining in school. Nine girls had missed significant amounts of schooling through non-attendance (self-exclusion). Two of these nine were among those who had experienced permanent exclusion.

In short, over half of the girls (n23) had been subject to some form of exclusion, either as a disciplinary sanction or through processes of self-exclusion. The remainder were generally judged by their teachers to be those who were regular school attenders who had not encountered difficulties. As we later uncovered, this was not necessarily the case for all. Some reported difficulties which had a significant impact on their learning but which had gone unreported and/or undetected.

All but one of the girls reported truanting for at least one day. Those we record as self-excluding (n9) are girls that regularly truanted over an extended period, usually several terms. Of these nine, two were being educated in pupil referral units (PRUs), three were attending further education colleges, one was in the mainstream school from which she had truanted and three had transferred to new schools. Attendance at both PRUs and colleges was part-time.

Contents

Part 1 of *Girls and Exclusion* consists of two chapters exploring the educational and broader policy contexts in which policies and practices relating to exclusion from school are taking place. Chapter 1 examines British government and international agendas relating to social exclusion and educational 'underachievement'. We argue that boys' needs have been prioritised over those of girls and that links between educational exclusion and crime have contributed to a moral panic about boys' social and educational exclusion. Consequently, socially and educationally excluded men and boys have been constructed as a threat to society. We examine how these issues have been portrayed in the media and in public discourse. Although significant numbers of girls and women are living in poverty and are effectively excluded from full participation in society, their responses to their situation mean that they are not usually perceived as a threat to the stability of their communities. The social and educational needs of girls and young women have therefore slipped down the policy agenda. The chapter draws on data from Britain and New Zealand to illustrate these phenomena. It also shows how such debates about boys' educational achievement have an impact in low-income countries, where they serve to undermine discourse and policy relating to gender equity and sensitivity. The limited opportunities of girls and women in these societies are thus further undermined.

In chapter 2 we examine the British government's policies relating to school exclusion and social exclusion. We trace how official discourse has changed during the period since 1997 when the Labour government came to power. We examine the relationship between this discourse and professional attitudes and cultures within education. We look, in particular, at the ways in which concern about youth violence has impacted on education policy and consider what this means in terms of meeting the specific needs of girls and ensuring their right to education. We analyse recent policy developments in the context of children's rights.

The chapter further explores educational policy developments, focusing on global interdependence, democratisation, competition and co-operation. We note how exclusion from school reflects and reinforces racial inequalities in education. We draw on the findings of our research to argue for a re-definition of exclusion from school, so that it encompasses self-exclusion, withdrawal from learning and truancy as well as disciplinary exclusion. It is only when we acknowledge that girls may respond differently from boys to difficulties at school that the full extent of their needs can be identified. We propose a re-definition of school exclusion so as to encompass girls' varied experiences and develop appropriate policy responses.

In part 2, *Girls In and Out of School*, we draw on the voices of girls and young women, exploring and analysing their experiences of inclusion and exclusion from school. We also examine the perspectives of professionals from a range of backgrounds who work with young women who are either out of school or who are judged to be vulnerable to exclusion. Chapter 3 identifies inequalities in resource allocation and access. We consider the processes by which disadvantaged and 'disaffected' youth are identified and their needs assessed. We review the services provided by agencies such as local authorities, colleges and voluntary organisations, which target those who are vulnerable to exclusion or who have dropped out of school. We demonstrate that resources that go towards supporting disaffected students and towards reducing exclusion and truancy are disproportionately targeted at boys. We examine why this happens, analysing the experiences and perspectives of the girls in our study and of the professionals who work with them.

In chapter 4 we examine how girls manage their schooling, exploring the concepts of success and survival. We report on girls' aspirations and their expectations of school in terms of examinations and future employability. We examine the pressure to succeed and the organisational and structural barriers, processes and procedures that need to be negotiated by students in order to survive the everyday experience of school. We consider how girls react when things go wrong, for example, when they encounter problems of bullying, racism or difficulties in learning or in relationships with their peers. We report on the strategies which girls adopt and the people they turn to for help, considering the role of family and friends. Strategies such as withdrawal from learning and truancy, as well as conflicts with teachers are discussed, together with their consequences.

Chapter 5 reports on girls' views of exclusion as a disciplinary sanction and on their views of what makes an inclusive school. We consider their views on their responsibilities and those of their teachers and the ways in which discipline is applied in schools. We also look at some of the alternatives to mainstream education and the ways in which they can serve to be inclusionary or exclusionary in their practices and outcomes. Issues such as 'girls-only' spaces and opportunities are discussed. Although many girls report that they flourish in alternative schemes, they also note that not all aspects of alternative education are helpful. We draw conclusions on how mainstream education might be made more inclusive.

In chapter 6 we examine the barriers to achievement that girls face. We report on aspirations, caring responsibilities, pregnancy, sexual vulnerability and peer relationships. Service providers discuss the various factors which they perceive to affect different groups of girls, focusing on the impact of ethnicity and social class. They highlight the lack of provision for girls and consider the particular needs of girls from different communities. Policy issues relating to informal exclusion and the use of further education colleges for under-16s are discussed.

Finally, in part three, *Including Girls*, we examine the practice and policy implications of our research for school, alternative education providers and government. School effectiveness debates and a focus on raising achievement, as defined in terms of improved public examination results, have been given high priority on the international educational policy agenda. We review what we have learnt from girls and stress how learners can make a positive contribution to the realisation of more effective schools.

Schools may be faced with an apparent dilemma in seeking to be inclusive of 'difficult' young people and those in difficulties. Pressures to improve attainment and respond to challenging boys may serve to mask girls' difficulties. We suggest how schools can become more inclusive of girls, enabling them to feel a genuine sense of belonging and achievement. Our research reveals a hidden problem of exclusion among girls. Given the link between poor attendance and poor achievement, policies aimed at reducing disaffection and promoting achievement will also need to address some of the specific causes of non-attendance among girls. A more inclusive school culture does not imply a less 'effective' school. We argue that if schools address the needs of those girls who are currently excluded, they are also likely to improve their overall examination performance.

In conclusion, we review the arguments for keeping girls as well as boys at the centre of the educational policy agenda, in order to achieve genuine social and educational inclusion. We highlight some contradictions and tensions between policy and practice. For example, education systems may have inclusionary policies, but exclusionary practices. We review what is meant by school effectiveness and note how schools celebrated for outstanding examination results may simply exclude poor performing pupils. We re-evaluate current practices in the light of what the girls in our study have told us about what makes a school more effective for them.

Part I

The policy context

Chapter 1

Girls: not a problem?

Over a five-year period, from 1995 to 1999, in England alone, over 10,000 secondary school-aged girls were permanently excluded from school as the result of disciplinary procedures. This amounts to the equivalent of the population of a small town. In this chapter we begin by drawing attention to the scale of the problem. Second, we stress how these officially recorded disciplinary exclusions are the tip of an iceberg, hiding a much wider and complex problem of girls' exclusion from school. Third, we demonstrate how girls' exclusion often has long-term harmful consequences because of when it occurs.

Officially recorded, permanent exclusions form a small proportion of the total numbers. Many more students are subject to fixed-term disciplinary exclusions or are unofficially excluded, as when parents are asked to find an alternative school for their daughter. Yet others engage in a form of self-exclusion, when they withdraw from learning, perhaps truanting but sometimes remaining physically present in school. Despite these various forms of exclusion, very little attention has been given to their impact on the lives of girls and young women. Most disciplinary exclusions (over 80 per cent) are from mainstream secondary schools and about two-thirds of the total number of excluded pupils are aged 13–15 years. They are expelled from school during the period leading up to public examinations, with potentially devastating consequences for their future. Girls make up one in four of all students excluded at this stage in their school careers. They are therefore a very significant minority. Although the government aims to provide permanently excluded pupils in England with alternative full-time education from 2002, many young people will drop out of school altogether or reach the official school-leaving age before these plans can be implemented.

Despite the British government's stated commitment to develop policies and practices which promote social inclusion, and official recognition of direct links between exclusion from school and social exclusion (Social Exclusion Unit, 1998), there has been little consideration of the specific needs of girls. Girls are still not taken seriously; boys are the cause for concern. Most policy-makers appear to have accepted the dominant discourse that girls are succeeding at school. Rather than acknowledge a problem of 'underachievement' and exclusion which affects both boys and girls, albeit in different forms, concern has continued to focus on 'underachieving' boys. There has been a distinct lack of interest in the problem of girls' exclusion from school, from policy-makers, research funding bodies and professional groups. When we set out to research girls' exclusion from school, a number of funding bodies indicated that as girls form a minority of excluded students, this was not a priority issue. And when we started the project the initial response from the majority of professionals whom we approached reflected this perspective: girls are simply 'not a problem'.

The launch of our research report *Not A Problem? Girls and school exclusion* (Osler *et al.*, 2002) in January 2002 attracted considerable media attention. Our study was not only reported in the educational press, but was also featured in a wide range of national newspapers, various BBC and independent radio news bulletins, BBC Radio 4's *Woman's Hour* and on BBC television's *Breakfast News*. The research, funded by the Joseph Rowntree Foundation, draws on girls' own perceptions of school life, their perceptions of the ways in which exclusion occurs and their strategies for resolving problems. In this chapter we consider various features of recent media constructions of girls' and boys' experiences and achievements at school. We reflect on the ways in which the media accounts of our research followed some of these established patterns and on how they differed from other recent media stories.

Although education policy debates have been prominent in England in recent years, with the government engaging in a range of consultation exercises, young people's voices have not been prominent in these debates. It was for this reason that we designed our research in such a way that girls' perspectives on inclusion and exclusion would be at the heart of our project. Our research sample included girls and young women who were judged by their teachers to be doing well at school as well as some who had been excluded or were thought to be at risk of exclusion. A total of 81 girls were interviewed individually and in small groups. We also sought out the opinions of a range of professionals from education, health, social services and voluntary sector agencies. We investigated a number of alternative education schemes aimed at those who, for various reasons, were not in mainstream education.

Some previous research examining girls' experiences of disruption in one mixed inner-city secondary school concluded:

> There is much to be learned from hearing what girls have to say for themselves. Teachers' and theorists' views do not reflect the complexity, the detail, the level of insight, the vigour and the feelings that girls express when they talk about their experiences. . . . Reflecting on and talking to girls and about girls should not be seen as a luxury item. They deserve an equal place in the spotlight.
>
> (Crozier and Anstiss, 1995: 31)

We concur with this viewpoint and argue that there are three specific reasons why girls' views and perspectives should be incorporated into developments in educational research, policy and pedagogy. These correspond to what we might call the three Ps, namely, principle, policy and pedagogy. First, the UN Convention on the Rights of the Child 1989 (CRC) sets an important international standard on the participation rights of children and young people and has wide ranging implications for education policy and practice (see, for example, Newell, 1991; Lansdown and Newell, 1994; Osler and Starkey, 1996; Verhellen, 2000). We argue that girls' viewpoints and perspectives need to be incorporated into educational research in recognition of the *principle* of young people's participation as set out in the CRC. Adherence to this principle has direct implications for policy and pedagogical practices.

Secondly, research projects which draw on young people's perspectives have the potential to inform and influence *policy*. Research which has drawn on the voices of young people from marginalised groups, such as children with special educational needs or girls from specific minority ethnic groups, have sometimes challenged the assumptions of education professionals concerning those groups (Osler, 1989; Tisdall and Dawson, 1994). Such approaches provide policy-makers with the opportunity to hear and to take into account the voices of otherwise marginalised young people. This was certainly one of the goals in carrying out

this study. In a sense we may even claim that these girls are enabled
to influence policy and practice. By seeking out the views of young
people, including young children, researchers may uncover how
social processes and educational practices operate to exclude or
discriminate against certain groups (Troyna and Hatcher, 1992;
Connolly, 1998).

Thirdly, research and consultation with children and young
people may also inform *pedagogy* and enable teachers to find practical solutions to everyday challenges facing schools. For example,
researchers have shown how such consultation processes inform and
strengthen school improvement strategies and support schools in
addressing questions of discipline (Ruddock *et al.*, 1996; Osler,
2000). As Crozier and Anstiss (1995) point out, the focus of attention has long been on boys' disruption. They argue that the Elton
Report (Elton, 1989) legitimised this emphasis since it identified
'verbal abuse' towards teachers, 'physical destructiveness' and
'physical aggression' as the most serious problems; this emphasis on
physical and noisy behaviour prioritises predominantly male
behaviour. Our study seeks to redress the balance by focusing on
girls' behaviour and their experiences of inclusion and exclusion at
school. The girls in our study suggest how pedagogical and school
organisational practices might be improved to enable greater
inclusion.

Gender, schooling and the media

The issue of exclusion from school is closely linked to that of
achievement; students who are barred from school or who absent
themselves for significant periods of time are unlikely to realise their
full academic potential. Not only will they miss key lessons but they
may also experience loss of self-esteem and/or difficulties reintegrat-
ing into school life which are likely to have both direct and indirect
impact on attainment.

Since the early 1990s, in Britain the media have drawn attention to
boys' 'underachievement' in public examinations, first at General
Certificate of Secondary Education (GCSE) level, which marks the
end of compulsory schooling at 16 years, and then at General Certificate of Education Advanced level (GCE A level), the examinations required for university entrance, normally taken at age 18.
The impression given is that girls have overtaken boys in what is
often unquestioningly presented as a competition between the sexes.

This is illustrated in such headlines as 'Girls on top form' (the *Guardian*, 6 January, 1998), 'It's a girl's world – they beat boys in best-ever exams' (the *Sun*, 20 August, 1999).

Girls' academic achievements are turned on their head. Instead of being seen as a cause for satisfaction, they are presented in the media and in popular discourse as a widespread problem of failure among boys, about which the educational community in general, and teachers in particular, should concern themselves. The improvement in the examination success of (some) girls provokes concern about boys, whose improvement rates are slower. Indeed, an article by a prominent academic in the *Times Educational Supplement* asserted: 'it is the under-achievement of boys that has become one of the biggest challenges facing society today' (Wragg, 1997: § 2 p. 4). Effectively, girls' relative examination success becomes a contributory factor in what is portrayed as a crisis of masculinity.

Table 1.1 draws on official statistics (DfES, 2001a) to show the relative performance of girls and boys at GCSE level over the three-year period 1998/99 to 2000/01. In 1999/2000, for example, 54.6 per cent of girls obtained five or more of the top (A*–C) GCSE grades compared with 44 per cent of boys. Girls' average achievement was thus more than 10 percentage points ahead of that of boys. Media attention focuses on the majority of girls (54.6 per cent) who achieve the top-grades. Government and media concern is expressed about the majority of boys (56 per cent) who fail to get these grades. Very little of the public discourse addresses the substantial minority of girls (45.4 per cent) who are also leaving school with less than five top-grade GCSEs. These girls, who are less likely than their male peers to have attracted attention to themselves by engaging in behaviour which leads to disciplinary exclusion, are nevertheless leaving school without marketable qualifications. In the eyes of many professionals they are simply 'not a problem'.

The discourse is about boys' 'underachievement' in relation to

Table 1.1 Percentage of female and male students attaining grades A* to C in GCSE examinations

Year	Girls	Boys	All students
1998/99	53.4	42.8	47.9
1999/00	54.6	44.0	49.2
2000/01	55.2	44.6	49.8

girls; the categories 'boys' and 'girls' are monolithic and there is little recognition of the vast differences in achievement which exist between girls and between boys, according to class and ethnicity (Epstein *et al.*, 1998; Griffin, 2000). It has been demonstrated that the 'gender gap' between the average attainments of boys and girls in GCSE examinations is, in fact, much smaller than those associated with ethnic origin and social class (Gillborn and Mirza, 2000). The girls' success story reflects improving examination success rates among particular groups of girls: those girls that are now out-performing their male peers are largely from middle-class back-grounds (Plummer, 2000; Walkerdine *et al.*, 2001).

The apparent success of girls at school is not necessarily reflected in post-school experiences. Mirza's (1992) study of African Carib-bean girls in London showed that even when they adopted strategies to succeed at school and achieve examination success, they were subsequently disadvantaged as they moved into the labour market. In Australia, 12 per cent more girls than boys complete secondary school. Among students who complete Year 12, girls achieve a higher average performance in most subjects in most states. Yet school success does not guarantee girls an advantage in the labour market. Researchers found that:

> Taking boys as a single grouping and comparing them with girls as a grouping, concern for boys' life chances on the basis of their schooling performance is misplaced. There is surprisingly little carry-over effect from the average girl's better performance . . . Indeed, the only evident effect is that a somewhat higher percentage of young women are proceeding to higher education. Boys' lower achievement levels in Year 12 subjects and even their lower level of literacy have no evident depressing effects in their employment chances if we are looking for effects across males as a single grouping.
>
> (Collins *et al.*, 2000a: 39)

In England there are also considerable differences in the relative achievement of each ethnic group across local education authorities (LEAs), with the percentage of 'Black Caribbean' heritage students achieving 5 or more A*–C grades ranging between 16 per cent and 59 per cent, depending on the LEA. It is unlikely that these vari-ations in achievement can be explained solely in terms of class; more research is required to understand the specific strategies and related resource allocation which is enabling some schools and LEAs to narrow the attainment gap between ethnic groups. Despite efforts to address differentials in attainment, there is still considerable inequality: in 2000, just 27 per cent of Black Caribbean heritage students obtained five or more of the top (A*–C) GCSE grades. These students were thus more than 20 percentage points below the national average (Tikly *et al.*, 2002).

International studies confirm the importance of considering the intersection of ethnicity and gender in order to understand achievement. Alton-Lee and Praat (2001), drawing on the IEA Third International Mathematics and Science study (Garden, 1997) and a study of literacy (Wagemaker, 1993), found that Year 5 students in New Zealand scored well above the international average in literacy, well below in mathematics and approximately equal in science. Nevertheless, they noted that achievement differed more by ethnicity than by gender.

Unfortunately, the official statistics for England do not allow us to examine gender differences within each ethnic group, as the Department for Education and Skills has not required LEAs to provide this breakdown. This is a curious and significant omission, given the general official concern about gender differences in achievement. It may reflect a more widespread trend among government officials and agencies often to overlook the intersection of gender and ethnicity when addressing questions of achievement.

When differences in achievement between ethnic groups are ignored and when assumptions are made about the homogeneous nature of the categories 'girls' and 'boys', the issue of which boys or girls may be underachieving, which boys or girls are causing concern, and which boys and girls are needing additional support is obscured. For example, when we conducted research into the ways in which OFSTED, the school inspection agency for England, was carrying out its government-assigned role for monitoring how schools were addressing and preventing racism, we noted that a number of senior OFSTED personnel gave race equality a low priority. One member of the OFSTED senior management team told us: 'Race equality is not a priority. Our priority is underachieving white boys'. Although this stated priority was subsequently denied by the chief inspector of schools (Osler and Morrison, 2000: 58), the comment makes explicit what is often not stated, that public discourse about male 'underachievement' is often in fact about *white* male 'underachievement'.

Black boys' 'underachievement' or exclusion from school only becomes part of the discourse when the area of policy broadens to include questions of social cohesion, crime and violence. Researchers, black families and communities have long been concerned about the failure of schools to recognise and realise the academic potential of black children, both boys and girls (see, for example, Coard, 1971; Troyna, 1984; Eggleston *et al.*, 1986). Popular concern about (white) boys' 'underachievement' is much more recent. Not only was the OFSTED leadership unwilling to recognise race equality as an essential element in its campaign to raise standards, it also appeared unconcerned that significant numbers of girls might be 'underachieving'. Media and professional obsession with boys' 'underachievement' and the success of some girls obscures the educational difficulties of a significant number of other girls.

From Table 1.1 we can see that both sexes have continued to show improvements in examination results in the three-year period from 1998/99 to 2000/01, but girls, as a group, are generally outperforming boys. The official statistics also confirm that among 17–18-year-old students taking A and AS levels, girls are outperforming boys, with an overall higher point score[1] (see Table 1.2). The picture can be seen

Table 1.2 Average point score for 17–18 year olds entered for GCE A and AS levels in schools and FE sector colleges, 2001

Students	Number entered	Average point score
Females	122,205	18.0
Males	107,275	17.3
Total	229,480	17.7

to be more complicated if we consider examination results in particular school subjects. As Murphy and Elwood (1998) show, children's learned gender preferences lead them to respond differently to different school subjects, which in turn leads to differential GCSE outcomes and access to particular A level subjects. Recent statistics confirm their findings that at A level, certain GCSE trends are reversed. For example, in 2001 around one in five of the students entering the traditionally male subject of A level physics was female (5,935 girls out of a total number of 27,704). Yet these few girls enjoyed a statistically significant higher success rate, 92 per cent, compared with 89 per cent for boys (DfES, 2001a). Such findings are replicated in New Zealand where far fewer girls than boys study sixth-form physics, but this relatively small number achieve a mean score of 63 per cent – considerably higher than the overall mean of 50 per cent (Alton-Lee and Praat, 2001).

Before the 1990s, the average performance of boys was better than that of girls in both sets of examinations. Yet this inequality seems to have been largely unquestioned, both by the media and by the academic community in general, the only exception being a small number of feminist academics (for example, Spender and Sarah, 1980; Weiner, 1985). The relative silence that existed when boys were generally outperforming girls suggests that this was somehow seen as normal or natural, whereas when girls started to outperform boys, there was suddenly a cause for concern (Arnot *et al.*, 1996; Epstein *et al.*, 1998).

Gender and exclusion

Media representations of school exclusion have been constructed in the context of a more general concern about disaffected youth. Youth is, of course, a gendered concept, and most media portrayals of disaffected youth have highlighted examples of boys' disaffection. In England, the official statistics suggest that around 83 per cent of those permanently excluded from school for disciplinary reasons are boys (DfES, 2001b). From such statistics it is easy to conclude that exclusion is largely a male problem. Yet, this is to ignore the significant numbers of girls permanently excluded from school each year; at the peak age for exclusion, 14–15 years (Year 10), one in four permanently excluded students is female (DfES, 2001b).

An examination of media coverage of a number of cases of exclusion in the mid-1990s (Parsons, 1999) revealed the tendency to emphasise the violent nature of the excluded students and the danger they posed to other students and to teachers. One such 13-year-old was repeatedly referred to as violent and a 'thug' by a number of national newspapers, with one paper characterising the student's family as 'The Family from Hell' (Parsons, 1999: 130–1). All the examples cited from the media are of boys and this reflects the general tendency of the media to portray school exclusion, more or less exclusively, as something which happens to boys.

Media portrayal of disaffected male youth and their vulnerability to exclusion from school is also reflected in policy initiatives. The House of Commons Select Committee on Education and

Employment presented a detailed summary of the evidence on disaffection in its fifth report covering the 1997/98 session of parliament. The report focused on young people excluded from the benefits of education, whether by absenteeism, formal or informal exclusion from school or by failure to achieve basic skills and minimum formal qualifications. These young people were estimated to be 8 per cent of all 14–16 year-olds and between 9 and 16 per cent of 16–19 year-olds. They are characterised as predominantly male and disproportionately from African Caribbean backgrounds. The report makes a direct link between criminality and school exclusion, asserting that this group of young people includes 'a high proportion of young offenders' and 'a high prevalence of risk-taking behaviour' such as smoking, drugs and early sexual activity (House of Commons, 1998).

There appears to be a strong link between school exclusion and juvenile crime; a study conducted for the Home Office found that 98 per cent of boys and 61 per cent of girls who were excluded from school admitted to offending (Graham and Bowling, 1995). A study by the Audit Commission (1996) found that 42 per cent of offenders of school age had been excluded from school and another by the Metropolitan Police found that 35 per cent of juveniles arrested were accused of a crime which had taken place during school hours (Gilbertson, 1998). There is a tendency in many countries to see youth as an indicator of the social health of the nation (Griffin, 1993; Wynn and White, 1997). The moral panic around male youth crime, together with the higher numbers of boys permanently excluded from school as a disciplinary offence, has led commentators to present the whole issue of school exclusion as another element in the crisis of masculinity.

Neglected girls? Media responses

When our research report was launched on 9 January 2002, three of the six national newspapers which covered the story chose to emphasise how girls' needs have been overlooked as a result of a focus on boys. This was a new media message and a significant departure from what had been, until that point, an almost exclusive concern about boys, focusing particularly on boys' academic 'underachievement', over the previous ten years. Before the launch of our report, few, if any, concerns had been expressed about girls, although their successes had been constructed in some newspapers as something rather unusual, requiring an explanation.

Under the headline 'Excluded girls overlooked by schools', the *Guardian* began by highlighting how the number of excluded girls is underestimated. According to the paper's education correspondent, girls were ignored as a result of a policy focus on boys' achievement and disaffection, within schools, local education authorities (LEAs) and central government. The *Guardian* report highlighted girls' problems at school, their caring responsibilities at home and the link between 'self-exclusion' and bullying. The *Independent* and the *Daily Telegraph* followed a similar line, but both tended to place the blame more squarely on schools and on teachers. The opening paragraph in the *Daily Telegraph*, under the headline 'Excluded girls are slipping the school net', thus began: 'The problem of girls being excluded from schools is going unrecognised because teachers are concentrating too heavily on unruly boys' (the *Daily Telegraph*, 9 January 2002: 5). Under a headline which also made reference to 'unruly boys', the *Independent* concluded that: 'Girls bullied at school dropped out or were expelled because teachers failed to notice their unhappiness and focused all their attention on disruptive boys' (the *Independent*, 9 January 2002: 7).

Thus, the problem is presented in either/or terms. Girls are neglected because boys are getting, or demanding, all the attention. There is no recognition that it might be in the best interests of all students for teachers to concern themselves with both girls and boys. Teacher attention and concern is thus seen to be a limited resource, which if spent on boys, is inevitably going to be at the expense of girls. Both papers raised the issues of bullying and truancy and discussed ways in which the official exclusion statistics hide a greater problem.

All three papers quoted a spokesperson for the Department for Education and Skills who asserted that the government was providing '£178m this year to help tackle poor behaviour and provide education outside school for excluded pupils – 33 per cent higher than 2000–01 and a tenfold increase on 1996–97'. None of the journalists seem to have questioned what proportion of these resources was being made available to girls, an unfortunate oversight, given our report's claim that a disproportionate number of schemes are targeted at boys and that there is no monitoring to see how this money is being allocated.

Whereas the *Guardian* suggests a systemic problem and the *Daily*

Telegraph and the *Independent* tend to blame teachers and schools, the *Sun* places total responsibility for the problem on girls themselves. Following a headline 'Girls' bully shame', the paper declares:

> Girls are to blame for a sharp rise in bullying and bad behaviour in schools, a report reveals today. They are being expelled in record numbers after shedding their 'goody' image – and wreaking havoc while teachers spend their time cracking down on boys.
>
> More than 1,800 girls were banned from lessons last year – and the number is rising fast. But experts believe the crisis is being IGNORED because heads believe girls are 'not a problem'. . . . many are getting off scot-free by using 'sneak tactics' against classmates.
>
> (The *Sun*, 9 January 2002)

The paper goes on to characterise different forms of violence and bullying in which boys and girls indulge. The story is interesting in that it follows the established route of blaming girls. This time they are not blamed for boys' 'underachievement' but for 'the crisis' of 'bullying and bad behaviour' in schools. The paper concludes its story with the comment that 'black girls are four times as likely to be expelled as those who are white', which, in the context of the *Sun*'s interpretation of events, suggests that black girls must take a considerable share of the blame for this crisis in schooling.

The *Independent* and the *Daily Telegraph* (but not the *Guardian*) also mentioned issues of race and ethnicity. The former pointed out how 'Afro-Caribbean girls' were 'nearly four times more likely to be expelled than white girls' and the latter noted that truancy data were not monitored by race or sex. Neither paper developed these points. By contrast, *The Times* and the *Mirror* placed black girls at the heart of their stories. The *Mirror*, with its headline 'Black girl class hell' (9 January 2002) focused exclusively on black girls, reporting problems such as bullying, racism and school drop-out 'due to harassment'. *The Times*'s education correspondent, under the headline: 'Black girls at risk of expulsion', claimed that: 'The study says that the problem of misbehaviour among girls of every ethnic group is being neglected, leading to a 'disaffected generation' (*The Times*, 9 January 2002: 7).

The Times's report was linked to another story, focusing on Labour MP Diane Abbott, who was said to have made the claim that 'the lack of strong black male role models for black boys was leading to high drop-out rates'. The story was more sensational than the other three broadsheets in its reference to a 'disaffected generation' and in a number of stereotypes, including 'bitching' by girls and the notion that black boys were failing as a result of a 'lack of strong black male role models'. There is very little in this discourse to suggest the intersection of gender and ethnicity in explaining the higher exclusion rate of black girls, although female teachers (both white and black?) were presented as complicit in the processes that had led to black boys' 'high academic drop-out rates' (*ibid.*).

The assertion that boys' 'underachievement' or poor behaviour is caused by the feminisation of teaching is not something which is supported by research. International research into literacy found that those countries with the highest average achievements also had the highest proportions of female teachers (Elley, 1992). It is arguable whether current school practices favour female learners. Although textbooks published since 1990 tend to avoid some of the worst excesses of sexist language which were a feature of many books as recently as a decade earlier (Osler, 1994), there is no evidence to suggest any feminist, or indeed female, bias in the school curricula. Delamont (1999) points out that boys tend to receive more teacher attention than girls and that female teachers tend to value boys' achievements more than those of girls. Indeed, research in a boys' school indicated that students saw a direct link between the relatively harsh discipline imposed by certain male teachers and the violent and anti-social school behaviour of significant numbers of students (Carter and Osler, 2000).

The article in *The Times* which sought to report on a specific group of girls, namely black girls, and to link their experiences both to other girls and to black male students, concludes with a comment from a teachers' union: 'Doug McAvoy, general secretary of the National Union of Teachers, said that there was a need for more black teachers but they were dissuaded from entering the profession because of poor working conditions' (*The Times*, 9 January 2002: 7).

This comment serves to obscure any specific reasons for the under-representation of black teachers within the profession. Effectively, it de-racialises the issue of teacher supply, recruitment and retention. There is no suggestion that 'poor working conditions' might refer to institutional discrimination and/or structural disadvantage or the 'everyday racisms' (Essed, 1991; Chebel d'Appollonia, 1998) of the classroom and staff room for which we have substantial evidence (CRE, 1988; Osler, 1997c). Instead, the reader is encouraged to focus on general difficulties in teacher recruitment.

The high exclusion rates of black students, both male and female, noted in *The Times*, were also picked up by at least one London radio station, which interviewed Diane Abbott alongside one of us, and by Radio 4's *Woman's Hour*, which gave 15 minutes to a discussion of our report. *Woman's Hour* presenter Jenni Murray introduced the feature by noting that 'the question about what to do with unruly pupils is back on the political agenda' and by reminding listeners that Diane Abbott was concerned:

> at the low-achievement and high-exclusion levels of young black males. She says the problem is caused by white female teachers who don't know how to handle them. It seems, she claims, that a black boy doesn't have to be long out of disposable nappies for some teachers to see him as a gangster rapper.
>
> (Jenni Murray, BBC 4 *Woman's Hour*, 8 January 2002)

Murray goes on to observe that 'while there is plenty of provision for bad boys, bad girls seem to be falling through the net'. The *Woman's Hour* feature included a pre-recorded report from a special school in Kent, in which the headteacher and several students spoke, which was followed by a live interview with one of us and the headteacher of a Manchester girls' secondary school. Jenni Murray drew on the report's findings to ask questions about the distribution of resources and facilities between boys and girls and about girls' access to alternative provision. The Kent headteacher spoke of the behaviour problems, 'serious disruptive behaviour' and non-compliance, which led girls to be referred to his school. He also noted that such girls generally had low self-esteem, experienced mood swings, and had a tendency to be promiscuous. The reference to promiscuity is interesting, as it is uncommon to find references to boys' sexual activity in professional discourses relating to youth disaffection.

Resources are likely to be distributed according to the ways in which professionals' perceive students' needs. If girls' difficulties are linked, for example, to their perceived sexual behaviour, with little reference to academic performance, whereas boys' needs are assessed by other criteria, this may influence referral rates to sources of support. For example, researchers who observed teachers' meetings called to discuss students' behaviour noted that the ratio of boys to girls claiming attention was 7:1. Moreover:

> Boys were almost invariably referred for under-achievement, reluctance to work, uncooperative and rude behaviour, bullying (victim or bully), fighting and criminal activity. Girls were most often referred for absence from school, health problems (particularly eating problems), victim of bullying, appearance (hair, dress, length of nails, jewellery), problems at home and relationships with boyfriends. It appears that boys are described in terms of their behaviour and academic performance, while girls are described in terms of their appearance and sexuality. . . . [T]here were also worrying examples of teachers reflecting inappropriately on girls' sexuality, e.g. 'she dresses like a tart', 'she knows more than she should'. Boys were not referred to in similar or equivalent terms.
>
> (Crozier and Anstiss, 1995: 36)

The *Woman's Hour* feature explored the intersection of race, ethnicity and gender in the treatment of girls at school. The Manchester headteacher, who had excluded a Muslim sixth-former for refusing to comply with the school's apparently flexible dress code, was asked in what circumstances she would use such a 'heavy-handed' tool as exclusion. She said she would exclude students for 'extreme behaviour', violence, disruption or intimidation, concluding that girls' behaviour could be 'more extreme' than that of boys but arguing that in her own 'multicultural' school there was a 'clear balance between the different races'. Moreover, she argued that the differentials in exclusion rates between different ethnic groups was 'more about behaviour than race', suggesting that exploration of racial inequalities was 'a tricky road to go down'.

This headteacher's observations relating to issues of gender, race and ethnicity demand further analysis. The notion that girls' behaviour can be 'more extreme' than that of boys may reflect a widespread tendency to judge girls' behaviour more harshly than that of boys when they are seen to move beyond what are regarded as acceptable feminine norms. So, for example, violence in girls may be judged to be 'extreme', whereas aggression and violence among boys, while not necessarily tolerated, may be seen as inevitable or 'natural'. As one of the professionals whom we interviewed for our research pointed out, girls, unlike boys, do not have the capacity to be 'loveable rogues'. Girls who misbehave are simply 'bad girls'. The label 'bad girl' often also carries direct or implied criticism of an individual's sexual behaviour. If teachers perceive or explain girls' behaviour in different terms from that of boys then they are likely also to respond differently to this behaviour. The Manchester headteacher's comment may reflect a more general 'boys will be boys' discourse among professionals working with young people (Epstein et al., 1998; Mills, 2001). The Kent headteacher develops the discourse further. He chooses to highlight girls' emotions, self-esteem and sexual behaviour. He does not portray loveable rogues: girls who fail to comply with certain norms are seen to be seriously disruptive and are clearly bad girls.

The Manchester headteacher's unwillingness to examine racial inequalities in education is somewhat disturbing. While we would not wish to adopt an essentialist position on questions of race and ethnicity, nor argue that racism is the sole explanatory factor in the differential exclusion rates which exist between black and white students of both sexes, we note that, for this headteacher, as for the union leader quoted above, racism is not even under consideration as an explanatory factor in the exclusion of black youth. Various studies have highlighted the ways in which teachers respond differently to students from different ethnic backgrounds (Gillborn, 1990; Wright, 1992; Connolly, 1998). Other studies have examined the ways in which exclusions are applied and experienced by black students (OFSTED, 1996; Osler, 1997a; Wright et al., 2000; Blair, 2001). There is also clear evidence that African Caribbean heritage students of both sexes are more vulnerable to exclusion as a disciplinary offence than their white peers (Gillborn, 1998; Osler and Hill, 1999). We contend that institutional racism needs to be considered as one explanatory factor in the higher exclusion rates of black students. Teachers need to be sensitised to the everyday racisms of school life and to their impact on minority ethnic students.

While it is now well established that students with special educational needs, in poverty and looked after by local authorities are also more vulnerable to exclusion (Hayden, 1997; Osler and Hill, 1999), this does not provide us with an adequate explanation of why 'Black Caribbean' students are between four and five times more likely to be excluded than those from other ethnic groups (DfES, 2001b). We know that exclusion rates vary widely between LEAs (Osler et al., 2000) and that black students are much more vulnerable to exclusion in some LEAs than in others. These variations are much greater than can be explained in terms of the socio-economic characteristics of the areas (Parsons and Howlett, 1995) or the class backgrounds of black students.

There were two other key national media reports of our research. The first was a substantial pre-launch feature in the *Times Educational Supplement* (Williams, 2002). Its title, 'Girls who give up', suggests that girls may be responsible for their own exclusion and for school failure, but the story, by drawing on the voices of a number of girls and young women who are accessing alternative education schemes, paints a different picture, one of isolated, bullied and emotionally distressed girls whose problems have gone unaddressed for some time. The article focuses on the underlying causes of truancy and on forms of exclusion, such as 'internal exclusion' where a student is banned from lessons but remains in school, which are not counted in the official overall exclusion figures. The writer tends to present girls as vulnerable victims rather than active agents, responding to the unfavourable conditions of schools.

Five weeks after the launch of our report there remained considerable media interest in the topic of girls' exclusion and behaviour. The *Independent* carried a substantial feature entitled 'Girl trouble: the hidden problem' which continued with a strapline explaining that 'concern about boys' achievement at school means that girls' needs are often overlooked. Some may be in desperate need of help' (Hinds, 2002: 6). This article is significant in that it marks a move away from previous modes of media reporting on gender, achievement and behaviour in school. The feature, which draws extensively from our report and on quotes from Cathy Street, one of our co-authors, sets the issue of girls' achievement alongside concerns about their behaviour, focusing on the problem of bullying amongst girls and on the need to provide support to address their emotional problems. The article challenges the previously accepted popular and professional discourses about boys' underachievement and girls' success:

> Bad boys have been hogging all the attention for too long. For the past six or seven years, boys' underachievement, boys' disaffection and boys' exclusion from school, have been constantly – not to say, obsessively – pored over by government ministers, Ofsted inspectors and the media. Girls, meanwhile, have been

sitting pretty, praised to the skies for their exam results, which have overtaken boys at GCSE and A-level.

But now, we are told, all is not well with the girls. Their academic averages conceal a significant pool of underachievement: in 2000, 14 per cent of 16-year-old girls had no qualifications. Girls are said to be suffering from bullying; they are engaged in self-destructive behaviour such as cutting themselves; and they are excluded from school officially and unofficially.

(Hinds, 2002: 6)

The *Observer* picked up the issue of girls and bullying in a full-page article in March 2002. Drawing on a range of research reports and intervention projects from the United States of America, the article argued that: 'Schoolgirls' ways of being cruel to each other are now so insidious and sophisticated that their victims can feel the devastating effects well into adulthood' (Hill and Helmore, 2002: 19).

The article also quoted extensively from our co-researcher, Cathy Street, and suggested that bullying amongst girls is now a widespread and serious problem in schools. It argued that girl-on-girl bullying is likely to lead not only to truancy and withdrawal but also to longer-term emotional and relationship problems. This article breaks with recent media reporting of gender differences and schooling. The spotlight is placed on girls and there is very little reference to or comparison with boys. The article marks a change of direction, with its focus on emotional problems and on relationships between girls. There is, however, no consideration of the implications of girls' friendships and bullying on their academic achievements. In some respects, however, established patterns are followed. Girls are portrayed as a homogeneous group; race, ethnicity and class are off the agenda. Consequently there is no opportunity to consider the ways in which these elements intersect. In particular, there is no acknowledgement or exploration of racial harassment or racial bullying.

Realising gender equity

Media representations of our research contrasted strongly with other recent media coverage of gender issues in education. The focus shifted from concern about boys' 'underachievement' and a need to explain girls' success, to a new emphasis on girls' behaviour and inclusion. Some stories blamed girls for their bad behaviour, others pointed the finger of blame at teachers and schools. Discerning readers might have identified a systemic problem and one which had developed out of an official policy focus on boys, but the research story, as reported, did not generally address the implications of this in terms of resource allocation. From a growing concern about boys' apparent disadvantage and a need to explain how girls as a grouping are outperforming boys as a grouping, the media switched to a concern about girls. We witnessed an example of what has been referred to as the 'gender see-saw' where girls are suddenly propelled into the spotlight. The sexes are compared and gender equity and justice are seen as 'a matter of balancing the books, evening up the score' (Collins *et al.*, 2000a: 38). As Collins and her colleagues note, and as we have argued in this chapter, this refocusing from boys to girls and back again is not, in itself, at all helpful. We need to understand the complexities of the situation and to work out which groups of girls are being included and/or achieving and which are not. Similarly we need to establish which groups of boys are doing well, remaining in much the same position or being excluded. Additionally, and importantly, we need to understand why these patterns are occurring, so that injustices can be addressed. In other words, 'we need to attend to the gender jigsaw in addition to the gender see-saw' (Collins *et al.*, 2000a: 38). Attempting to complete this complex jigsaw will involve looking beyond schools:

> [A] full understanding of gender justice in education requires a consideration of both the influences on and the consequences of school retention, participation, performance and outcomes. In this sense, attention must be paid to what students bring to school as a consequence of their 'backgrounds', what happens to them during school (their experiences, choices and performances), the credentials, knowledge, capacities and dispositions that they take with them when they leave school, and the value assigned by the labour market to what they take with them.
>
> (Collins *et al.*, 2000a: 38–9)

Our study seeks to make a modest contribution to the gender jigsaw by looking beyond the achievement data and seeking to understand girls' experiences of school, particularly their experiences of inclusion and exclusion. We argue that questions relating to friendship and to the quality of relationships between girls and the professionals with whom they work are critical, and that these are likely to have a direct impact on academic achievement as well as feelings of inclusion and belonging. For these reasons we draw on girls' own accounts of school life and those of a range of professionals to develop our understanding of the processes of inclusion and exclusion as they apply to girls. We also examine what happens to girls when their needs are not met in mainstream schooling and seek to establish what girls really want from school.

We suggest that these questions are not just critical for education policy in relatively prosperous 'First World' countries but also have implications for gender equity and justice in low-income countries. Around two-thirds of illiterate people in the world are women and differential illiteracy rates are both a direct reflection and an indicator of discrimination and women's restricted opportunities. A high illiteracy rate reflects a country in poverty and in some countries women and men have very similar high illiteracy rates. A more common pattern, however, is for women's illiteracy rates to be higher than men's. In over 40 countries world-wide the illiteracy rate for women is 20 or more percentage points greater than men's and in 19 countries it is higher than 75 per cent. Additionally, girls are still less likely to be enrolled in school and when they do enrol they drop out at an earlier age. They are held back by the assumption that educating them will be a waste (Seager, 1997).

Access to primary education is a basic human right, yet in most African countries, for example, female enrolment in primary schooling lags well behind male enrolment (UNESCO, 1995b; United Nations, 1995; Bloch and Vavrus, 1998). Structural Adjustment Programmes (SAPs) make it increasingly likely that girls will drop out of school at a very early age as parents, obliged to pay school fees and make other contributions to their children's schooling, prioritise the education of their sons over that of their daughters. Struggles by grassroots organisations to improve women's position have tended to focus on adult women, leaving the formal school system untouched. Pressures to achieve cost reduction in education and the increased costs of schooling affect men and women unequally, limiting the education of all girls except those from wealthy families (Stromquist, 1998). Girls' opportunities have therefore been undermined and are likely to be even further restricted. In this context, cries of 'What about the boys?' and concerns about boys' disadvantage are particularly damaging. At the International

Bureau of Education Africa Regional Conference *Learning to Live Together* in Nairobi in June 2001, when discussion of violence at school and girls' security was raised, a few participants responded by alleging that we should now be addressing boys' needs as they are now the disadvantaged group. It would appear that 'First World' concerns about boys' 'underachievement' have begun to spread to the poorest region of the world. In at least 26 sub-Saharan African countries, women's rates of illiteracy are 20 or more points greater than those of men. In fact, the island of the Seychelles is the only country in the Africa region where the illiteracy rate of men is marginally higher than that of women (Seager, 1997).

International aid and technical assistance for educational development programmes increasingly require these programmes to incorporate gender equity components. One common model of technical assistance has been that of placing expatriate resident experts to work alongside local counterparts. In principle, local workers are trained to take over when the expert leaves. However, the model often breaks down because local workers may not, in fact, receive appropriate training and the experts, who are usually better paid, may be judged by local counterparts as having a limited commitment to the country in which they are working (Kochhar, 1997). A further problem is that technical assistance sometimes involves exporting failed Western models of effective schooling to developing countries (Lynch, 1997). The relatively unchallenged notion that it is boys who are now disadvantaged in education and therefore deserving of additional support may be particularly well received in contexts where there is already suspicion that gender equity initiatives are undermining traditional beliefs and where economic insecurities threaten men's traditional employment opportunities.

In a British government-funded project in Kenya, which was designed to improve primary schooling, this model of expatriate experts, responsible for training local educators, was adopted. The project had gender sensitivity as one of its objectives. One of us (Audrey) was employed as a consultant to the project between June and September 1995 and so had the opportunity to work alongside participants and engage in training with a team of Kenyan colleagues. None of the British expatriates working on longer contracts and leading professional development programmes had any special expertise in the area of gender equity. The training had addressed gender questions within the context of the curriculum, notably in relation to the teaching of mathematics and science.

Among the Kenyan educators, broader discussion of gender issues and the participation of women and girls in training activities provoked a strong emotional reaction and a wide range of opinions. Sixty per cent of the men in the programme believed that women were disadvantaged in education, identifying it as both a moral and an economic issue. A number of them gave examples of ways in which they had sought to address this problem in their personal lives (generally by encouraging or supporting their daughters) but none had actively taken steps to promote gender equity as part of their responsibilities as primary school advisors and inspectors. It was only women who acknowledged gender equity as a professional responsibility and were willing to address beyond their own family contexts (Osler, 1997b), and they formed a small minority of participants on the programme. Participants identified community leaders and officials as major obstacles to the realisation of gender equity. Since they were often dependent on these same people for basic material support, such as the provision of accommodation and transport, it was not in their interest to raise difficult or contentious issues. It seems likely that unless professional development programmes are extended beyond curriculum concerns to address broader cultural questions and the practical challenges of implementing change in emotionally sensitive areas, gender equity goals are unlikely to be realised.

We have discussed how public debates which prioritise the needs of boys over those of girls and the media representations of these issues may serve to mask complex injustices and inequalities in education. These debates have had a considerable impact on policy initiatives in a range of international contexts. Our contribution to the 'gender jigsaw' is to examine the ways in which girls are included or excluded from school. Social inclusion is likely to depend, to a greater or lesser extent, on the degree to which students are included at school. The next chapter will examine the concepts of school inclusion and social exclusion as they apply to girls and young women.

Chapter 2

Re-defining inclusion and exclusion

School exclusion and social exclusion

In 1998 the British government published its report *Truancy and School Exclusion* which made explicit the direct link between exclusion from school and longer-term social exclusion. In this report the government set itself a 'tough but achievable' target of a one-third reduction in the levels of both truancy and permanent and fixed-term disciplinary exclusions by 2002 (Social Exclusion Unit (SEU), 1998: 2). The report placed considerable emphasis on the relationship between truancy, exclusion and school failure, resulting in a subsequent lack of qualifications and unemployment. Although the report warned about the dangers of young people engaging in crime, the overall emphasis was on young people in difficulties, rather than on young people as the difficulty. The report acknowledged research which demonstrates wide variations in truancy and exclusion rates between schools whose populations experience similar socio-economic circumstances (OFSTED, 1996; DfEE, 1997; Osler, 1997a). It also recognised that some students were being excluded for minor incidents, which were never intended as grounds for exclusion, and that some others were excluded for more serious incidents which might be avoided or dealt with in other ways by schools. The message was clear – schools should not use exclusion or condone truancy as a routine means of coping with disaffected or failing students:

> Truancy and exclusions have reached crisis point. Thousands of children who are not in school on most schooldays have become a significant cause of crime. Many of today's non-attenders are in danger of becoming tomorrow's criminals and unemployed.

No one knows precisely how many children are out of school at any time because of truancy and exclusion. But each year at least one million children truant, and over 100,000 children are excluded temporarily.

. . . This damages the children themselves and everyone else: the children themselves lose out because they stop learning. This is self-evident for truants, but it is also a problem for excluded pupils. . . . These lost years matter: both truancy and exclusion are associated with a significantly higher likelihood of becoming a teenage parent, being unemployed or homeless later in life, or ending up in prison.

(Social Exclusion Unit, 1998: 1)

Addressing youth violence

From 1995/96, when school exclusions peaked at 12,467, official statistics indicated a downward trend in the annual number of permanently excluded students. This trend was reversed in 2000/2001. The 2000/2001 estimate of 9,210 permanent exclusions amounted to an increase of 11 per cent from the previous year. The government's original highly publicised reduction target had not been met. Yet Secretary of State for Education and Skills Estelle Morris was quoted as saying she was 'not too upset' about the increase: 'There has got to be a clear message to young people that behaviour is important. If boundaries are crossed, consequences take place' (Estelle Morris, Radio 4 *Today Programme*, 23 May 2002).

Official discourse had changed significantly. The emphasis was no longer on enabling social inclusion but on combating youth violence and crime. The new ministerial message was that an increase in school exclusions reflected a united approach by government and schools in response to violent and unruly behaviour. The message was reinforced by headlines such as 'School exclusions are up – to the delight of ministers' (the *Independent*, 24 May 2002: 19). A central feature of the government's plans to combat social exclusion – cutting the number of school exclusions – had disappeared. It had been replaced by growing official concern about the need to address youth violence and criminal behaviour, in which exclusion from school was seen as an essential policy tool. An increase in the number of exclusions was equated with the drive to improve 'standards' and with improved discipline in schools. Ministers promised that no further exclusion reduction targets would be set.

In fact, the British government's changing approach to exclusions did not mark a sudden change in policy but a developing response to a range of pressures, in particular from teacher unions, which were expressing concern that exclusion appeal panels were reinstating disruptive and violent pupils. As one union leader was quoted as saying, following the announcement of the rise in exclusions:

> [The statistics] reflect the reality of rising levels of pupil violence, disruption and abuse. Nobody should rejoice at today's figures. But it is far better for heads to be strongly supported in their defence of decent education standards than to be subjected to ridiculously artificial and damaging reduction targets.
>
> (David Hart, General Secretary of the National Association of
> Head Teachers, quoted in the *Independent*, 24 May 2002: 7)

An exclusionary culture

In August 2000 and again in January and May 2002 the government relaxed exclusion regulations, making it easier for headteachers to exclude students who were violent, persistently disruptive, or who were engaged in bullying or in drug dealing. In April 2002 the government completed a consultation exercise, which proposed further limitations to the exclusion appeal process. Without adequate rights of appeal, the measures to address bullying and drugs, which appear at first sight to be reasonable, are extremely problematic. As Labour MP Barry Sheerman, Chair of the House of Commons Education Select Committee, observed in relation to guidance which makes it easier to exclude a student accused of bullying: 'One stroke and you're out is pretty dramatic because sometimes you can be picking on the victim not the bully' (Barry Sheerman MP, Radio 4 PM, 16 January 2002, quoted on BBC News On Line).

One difficulty is that schools do not necessarily have to establish high standards of proof. Drug dealing is clearly a serious criminal offence and a student excluded for this offence will have this on his or her record. In effect, such a student will be criminalised, without necessarily having gone through any legal process and without the opportunity to challenge any injustice which may have occurred in the processes in operation at school. Appeal panels have been advised that they should not normally overturn an exclusion of this nature.[1]

There is considerable evidence that appeal panels were already strongly weighted in favour of schools (Harris and Eden, with Blair, 2000), and it is parents or guardians, rather than students themselves, who have rights of appeal. This means that young people who are looked after by local authorities may have no one who is able to act on their behalf. In reality, parents have very limited rights which only come into operation when a student is permanently excluded and when the exclusion is carried out according to the official guidelines. Children can be permanently excluded from school without having any opportunity to defend themselves, highlight an injustice or challenge the decision. Where a student is excluded informally, whether for a short period or indefinitely, parents may find that there is no clear way forward (Osler and Osler, 2002). If a headteacher excludes a student informally and fails to observe the statutory guidance on exclusion there is no clear or immediate means of redress. Evidence presented to the UN Committee on the Rights of the Child proposes that the right of appeal be extended to children, in order to comply with Article 12.2 of the Convention on the Rights of the Child (CRC) (Lansdown and Newell, 1994). Article 12.2 requires that children: 'be provided with the opportunity to be heard in any judicial or administrative proceedings affecting the child, either directly or through a representative or an appropriate body'.

Each of the rulings which make it easier for headteachers to exclude a student undermines the relatively progressive statutory guidance which was brought into effect following the publication of the Social Exclusion Unit's (SEU's) report on *Truancy and School Exclusion*. This guidance promoted a culture of inclusion rather than exclusion and brought together for the first time strategies on behaviour management and measures which might be taken when these strategies were ineffective (DfEE, 1999a and b). More recent ministerial pronouncements, focusing as they have on student violence and on exclusion for a first 'offence', contribute to a culture of exclusion, in which young people are readily stigmatised as belonging to a violent generation and liable to threaten teachers. Yet the government's own report on exclusions cited research which suggests that it is only in a small minority of exclusion cases where there is physical violence or where teachers are the victims of abuse (SEU, 1998). Ministerial pronouncements serve to legitimise exclusion as an option for those schools which enforce punitive discipline and which lack appropriate support for young people with learning, social or emotional difficulties.

Evidence-based policy?

Following the 1997 election, the new Labour government made a commitment to evidence-based policy development in education. The SEU report (1998: 23) stated 'the Government will commission a major research study on the reasons for exclusion'. We were commissioned to carry out this research in spring 1999. Our study set out to understand more about the events which lead to fixed-term and permanent exclusions, the procedures and practices which help minimise its use, and the characteristics of high and low excluding schools. Our research in six local education authorities (LEAs) and in schools within those authorities revealed the growing practice of unofficial exclusion by headteachers, which was often undetected by LEAs (Osler *et al.*, 2000). Official statistics, which suggest a decrease in permanent exclusions between 1996/97 and 1999/2000, mask an increasing use of fixed-term exclusions and of unofficial exclusions, both temporary and permanent, during this period.

One potentially constructive measure arising from the SEU report was the decision by the Prime Minister:

> to establish a Ministerial task force to review progress in tackling exclusion and truancy, and to monitor the follow up to this report. All relevant Departments should be represented. This will be chaired by the Minister for School Standards and make an annual report.
>
> (SEU, 1998: 27)

The establishment of the ministerial task force, as part of an effort to promote 'joined-up government', acknowledged the complexity of the issues behind truancy and school exclusion and the need for complex and comprehensive responses. We were invited to present the findings of our research to this task force in autumn 1999, but the presentation never took place. Our understanding is that no meetings of the ministerial task force took place between autumn 1999 and December 2000 when the DfEE finally published our research report. A year or so after the task force was established it had apparently stopped meeting. As we have seen, guidance that allowed headteachers more leeway in excluding students was introduced from August 2000. In autumn 1999, when our government-commissioned research into the underlying reasons for exclusion from school was complete, government rhetoric concerning school exclusions and long-term social exclusion was being maintained, but inclusionary policies and practices as proposed in the SEU report (1998) and statutory guidance (DfEE, 1999a and b) were already being undermined. Efforts to cut school exclusion were no longer a priority.

Discussion of violence and school exclusion serves to reinforce the notion that exclusion from school is, to a large extent, a male problem. The official links that have since been made between school exclusion and violence in schools underline claims of a crisis among boys. It is asserted that physical violence in schools is a largely male problem (Mills, 2001), despite concerns that it may be becoming more common among girls. As we seek to demonstrate in chapter 3, continued attention on excluded boys is likely to have an ongoing impact on resource allocation. A number of studies document programmes which seek to tackle violence amongst boys and enable them to accept a broader range of masculinities (for example, Salisbury and Jackson, 1996; Carter and Osler, 2000; Mills, 2001). Although we have come across 'anger management' courses targeted at girls, we are not aware of studies which document ways of addressing violence and aggressive behaviour among girls.

None of the recommendations in the SEU report addressed the specific needs of girls at risk of exclusion or truancy, although the report does make passing reference to pregnancy, noting that it 'is not in itself a sufficient reason for exclusion' (SEU, 1998: 9). Teenage pregnancy was, in fact, the subject of a subsequent report in which the relatively high rate of teenage pregnancy in the UK is explained in terms of the low educational and job market expectations of young mothers; ignorance about contraception, sexual health and the responsibilities of parenthood; and mixed messages about sex from the media on the one hand and families and public institutions on the other (SEU, 1999). The report presents the 90,000 teenage pregnancies which occur annually (8,000 to those under 16) as a problem. They are seen, almost inevitably, as leading to social exclusion:

> [T]he report is not just about what has gone wrong. It sets out how we can put it right. It contains a package of measures to help dramatically reduce the rate of teenage pregnancy in Britain and to tackle social exclusion among young parents and their families.
>
> It sets out what we are doing to improve education and job

opportunities. Most teenagers who are likely to become pregnant come from poor areas, and from disadvantaged backgrounds. Often they feel they have nothing to lose by becoming
pregnant. They badly need help at school and support to find
jobs and follow a career.
(Prime Minister Tony Blair in the introduction to SEU, 1999: 4)

Yet, Phoenix (1991) argues that early pregnancy is not, necessarily, a
problem:

> Contrary to popular belief and the ways in which 'teenage
> motherhood' has been socially constructed, early motherhood
> does not constitute cause for general concern. The majority of
> mothers investigated in this study (as well as in other studies)
> were coping with motherhood well. Their children . . . were also
> faring well.
>
> (Phoenix, 1991: 247)

The implication of the government report (SEU, 1999) is that
early motherhood is rarely, if ever, a sound or informed choice. Yet
typical choices about motherhood, marriage and life cycle patterns
vary between women of different social classes and (as the Social
Exclusion Unit report notes) ethnic groups. Researchers have noted
that while middle-class women tend to delay having children until
they have completed their education and become established in their
careers, some working-class women opt for early motherhood and
continue their education once their children have started school
(Walkerdine et al., 2001). Nevertheless, early motherhood does limit
educational opportunities for many. For those under 16 it commonly marks the end of their formal education. Nevertheless, it is
curious that a government which places considerable emphasis on
life-long learning should imply that women who delay having children until their thirties have necessarily made a wiser choice than
those who complete their higher education at this stage. Instead of
putting pressure on mothers who wish to care for their own young
children to take up training or employment, widening the educational and training opportunities for those women wishing to
return to study in their early and mid-twenties might equally resolve
problems of social exclusion.

Right to education

In certain countries, but by no means universally, exclusion from school is widely accepted as a means of disciplining those young people who are judged to be violent towards their peers, aggressive in their approach to teachers or who continually disrupt lessons. Messages about the need for school exclusion as a disciplinary tool are promoted by teacher unions and reinforced through the media. Government guidance on school exclusion often emphasises the 'benefits' of exclusion. For example, the New Zealand Ministry of Education explains:

> Stand-downs,[2] suspensions, exclusions and expulsions are essentially ways to deal with student behaviour that disrupts teaching and learning and threatens the well being of other students. These approaches are not used lightly by schools, but are part of a process to help students return to productive learning and relationships with the school community.
>
> (Ministry of Education, 2001)

In England, schools are advised that:

> A decision to exclude a child should be taken only:
>
> - in response to serious breaches of the school's discipline policy; and
> - if allowing the pupil to remain in school would seriously harm the education or welfare of the pupil or of others in the school; or
> - in most cases a range of strategies, including a Pastoral Support Programme, should have been tried and proven to have failed ... including considering whether the child's behavioural difficulties might arise from unmet special educational needs; or
> - where a pupil's action poses serious risk to the health and safety of the pupil or others in the school.
>
> (DfEE, 1999a)

As we can see, official guidance on exclusion confirms that disciplinary exclusion should generally only apply to students whose behaviour is seriously undermining the processes of teaching and learning. In other words, exclusion is seen as a legitimate disciplinary process if a student's behaviour causes an infringement of fellow students' right to education within a secure environment. Whereas it might be argued that a stand-down or fixed-term exclusion lasting a few days might enable both the student and the school to reflect on difficulties and come together to resolve these and re-establish good working relationships, claims that longer-term suspensions or exclusion from school are 'part of a process to help students return to productive learning and relationships with the school community' (New Zealand Ministry of Education, 2001: 3) are less credible. In practice students can be suspended for quite long periods, sometimes years (Darlow, 2001). A student suspended for a long period or permanently excluded from school is usually not in a position to maintain relationships with the school or any other learning community. In New Zealand the principal of the school from which a student is suspended/excluded must help them enrol in another school. However, the legislative framework permits schools to refuse to enrol students who have been excluded from other schools. Thus a student loses any right to education in the mainstream school environment.

According to official statistics, 15 per cent of those who experience a suspension in New Zealand drop out of school permanently or indefinitely: 6 per cent leave school, sometimes obtaining an official permit to do so at the age of 15 years; 5 per cent are awaiting enrolment elsewhere and the outcome for a further 4 per cent is unknown (Ministry of Education, 2001). Those who have been permanently excluded are even less likely to continue their education. Since other schools are not legally obliged to enrol them, many are left with no alternative other than to prematurely abandon their education or enrol in Correspondence School. The Correspondence School, which was originally set up to educate those living in remote areas, is unlikely to meet the needs of those young people whose emotional or behavioural difficulties are compounded by feelings of rejection as a result of exclusion. Nor can it meet specific social needs. Its retention and success rates for excluded students are low (Darlow, 2001: 28).

In England, many young people formally excluded from school have, until recently, received no education or very limited part-time provision, often restricted to less than four hours a week. The government promises access to full-time alternative education for certain categories of excluded pupils from September 2002, but as the Audit Commission (1999) has pointed out, LEAs may only realise this goal by prioritising the needs of formally excluded students over other groups: 'LEAs may be tempted to remove resources from those educated out of school for reasons other than exclusion, in order to provide full-time education for the excluded' (Audit Commission, 1999: 62).

If the Audit Commission's concerns prove to be justified, it is likely that girls will be disproportionately affected by this re-allocation of resources. Certain students, including school refusers, pregnant schoolgirls and young mothers, who have been educated in pupil referral units (PRUs) on a part-time or full-time basis, or who received some home tuition, may lose their right to education as LEAs re-direct resources to excluded students in line with government guidelines.

Since school enrolment is subject to market forces, it is often difficult for an excluded student to find an appropriate place in an alternative school. Successful schools are unlikely to have vacant places; students excluded from a special school and other students with special educational needs may find it difficult to find a school which can meet those needs, particularly if they have passed the statutory school-leaving age (Osler and Osler, 2002). The only vacant places may be at schools where attainment levels are well below the national average and where the staff are already struggling to meet the needs of students.

Disciplinary exclusion has become so widely accepted that a number of studies, including some of our own, have tended to focus on the disproportionate number of exclusions among students from particular ethnic groups or on ways of reducing exclusions more generally, without necessarily discussing whether exclusion is an acceptable practice (Osler, 1997a; Osler et al., 2000). In recognising the considerable challenges facing teachers, there is a tendency to accept some exclusions as unfortunate but necessary measures to enable the effective management of schools. In doing this, we may overlook the fact that other schools, often operating in similar and difficult circumstances, have avoided or minimised the use of exclusion as a disciplinary tool (Bourne et al., 1994; Osler, 1997a; Blair, 2001).

Some studies have focused on practical ways of preventing exclusions, demonstrating how students can be supported within existing frameworks or how practices can be modified so that schools become more inclusive (see for example, CRE, 1997; Cooper et al., 2000; Munn et al., 2000; Lloyd et al., 2001). Where the focus is on meeting the needs of individuals, there is sometimes a tendency to overlook or challenge systemic weaknesses. It is critical to remember that exclusion does not operate in a political vacuum. As we discuss below, policy and legislative frameworks which require schools to operate within a (quasi-) market, mean that some students, such as those with special educational needs or English as a second language, who are likely to cost more to educate, become less attractive to schools. These students may consequently find it more difficult to secure places at popular schools and become more vulnerable to exclusion from schools which fail to address their learning needs.

Debates about differential exclusion rates of different groupings of students continue to take place in a political vacuum. As we noted in chapter 1, headteachers may argue that the differentials simply reflect differences in behaviour, between boys and girls or between students from different ethnic groups. Not only do such debates overlook differential teacher expectations of students according to gender and ethnicity, they also fail to take into account underlying social inequalities. So, for example, in England, African Caribbean children of both sexes are more vulnerable to exclusion from school than their white peers. Such children are also from families which are, statistically, more likely to experience other forms of discrimination and disadvantage, in areas such as housing and unemployment. We suggest that such exclusions are not only a reflection of wider societal inequalities but are themselves an indicator of discrimination.

There is also little discussion of the immediate or longer-term psychological impact of exclusion. Exclusion leads to feelings of intense frustration and rejection. It is only when there is a tragedy, as when excluded student 19-year-old Robert Steinhäusser returned to his high school in Erfurt, Germany in April 2002 and killed 17 people, including 13 of his teachers, that we pause to consider the psychological damage an exclusion may cause. Steinhäusser, a persistent truant, was excluded from school just two months before he was due to sit his school-leaving examinations. In cases like this, which receive considerable media attention, the focus is less on the underlying causes of an individual student's difficulties, but on a more immediate concern, such as gun regulation laws. This serves to limit public debate on whether exclusion from school is an appropriate disciplinary procedure.

Rights in and through education

We argue that the issue of exclusion from school needs to be understood within the framework of human rights. Education needs to be
recognised as a basic right which should not be withdrawn from
those young people who experience social, behavioural or emotional difficulties. Education is not simply a right in itself, but one
which leads to other rights. It is helpful to consider rights *to*, *in* and
through education (Verhellen, 2000). Young people need to be recognised as citizens with rights, rather than citizens in waiting (Osler
and Starkey, 1996; Verhellen, 2000). They need to be informed
about their rights (rights through education) and to exercise them in
schools (rights in education).[3] The UN Convention on the Rights of
the Child (CRC) provides us with a framework in which we can
consider the expectations we place upon both teachers and learners.
Under the CRC, young people not only enjoy the right to education
but hold various rights *in* education, for example, the right to be
protected against discrimination and to be consulted in matters or
procedures which may affect them. They are able to access further
rights *through* education, such as rights to health and the skills which
enable them to claim their participation rights. This implies that
young people not only have access to education in human rights
through the taught curriculum but they are also able to experience
those rights as members of a school community who are listened to
and respected.

It is increasingly being recognised that a human rights framework
provides a sound basis for realising non-discriminatory practices in
a range of public services, enabling service providers and those
accessing the services to understand their common interests. The
police force provides an interesting example. In the UK, attempts to
enact the recommendations of the Stephen Lawrence Inquiry
(Macpherson, 1999), enabling the police to provide an appropriate
service to all citizens within multi-ethnic communities, have had a
mixed degree of success. This is despite the development of anti-
discrimination training and equality policies which have been characterised as 'far in advance of other state agencies' (Jasper, 2002). It
has been argued that what is needed is a full review of the police
training curriculum to 'reflect a broader curriculum, informed by an
integral philosophy of human rights, diversity and anti-discriminatory
practice' (ibid: 31, our emphasis).

We argue that teachers need education in human rights (Osler and

Starkey, 1996; Osler, 2000). In England, teachers' unions have presented the issue of exclusion as one of teachers' rights. They have
argued that teachers' rights are placed at risk by unruly students,
who threaten to undermine their ability to carry out their work in a
secure environment. Teachers need to be encouraged to consider
their own professional culture and the degree to which this enables
or undermines the rights of learners. This is critical if schools are to
become inclusive communities where the rights of both children
and teachers are maintained. Both public discourses relating to
young people and professional discourses of those who work with
them need to be informed by an integral philosophy of human
rights. Such a human rights framework permits us to look beyond
simple binaries in which the rights of teachers and learners are seen
as inevitably in conflict. When apparent or real conflicts arise, these
can often be resolved when systems, such as school councils, are in
place which allow learners to voice their concerns and to participate
in decision-making (Osler and Starkey, 1998; Carter and Osler,
2000). There is some evidence to suggest that a more democratic
school is likely to be a more disciplined school (Davies, 1998; Osler,
2000).

School councils and other mechanisms permit young people to
have a collective voice in school and to participate in decision-
making through their elected representatives. Such structures allow
students to develop key skills as citizens and complement the learning for citizenship which takes place through the formal curriculum
and in the community. Equally important to the setting up of school
councils and other mechanisms through which young people can
have a voice in school, is an educational legal and administrative
framework which allows individuals to be heard when things go
wrong. An important feature of any democratic structure is a means
of redress if an individual believes that their rights have been denied
or justice has not been done. Citizenship education, which has been
introduced as a national curriculum subject in England from 2002,
permits all young people to learn about democracy, participation,
rights and responsibilities. One of the underlying reasons for intro-
ducing this subject is a concern by politicians and others about a
democratic deficit among the young.[4]

We have argued above that the regulations governing exclusion
appeal panels need to be amended so as to bring them in line with
Article 12 of the Convention on the Rights of the Child and ensure
that those subject to disciplinary exclusion have the right to be

heard. Government and schools also need to review other administrative procedures to ensure that young people's voices are heard.
Unless this right is guaranteed students will identify the disjunction
between messages in the curriculum about citizenship and participation and the realities of the educational administrative and legal
frameworks which govern school life. This may serve to undermine
rather than reinforce young citizens' trust and commitment to
democratic processes. The goal must be for young people to experience citizenship as well as learn about it. As a lawyer, working to
support students who have been excluded, observes: 'Knowledge
about rights is not sufficient – knowing how to exercise those rights
is equally important' (Darlow, 2001: 6). To this we would add that
mechanisms to claim these rights are also essential.

Citizenship, democracy and inclusion

In the UK, the government has set out to raise standards of
achievement in education, so that learners will have the skills to
compete successfully in a world job market. Processes of globalisation and increasing levels of global interdependence are affecting
nearly all aspects of our lives. Considerable emphasis is placed on
the basic skills of literacy and numeracy for participation in the
wider economy and in society. The 2001 Education White Paper,
Schools Achieving Success, stressed accountability, inspection, meeting the needs of the individual, consumer choice and improved
incentives for teacher performance as the means by which educational standards can be raised in this global competition (DfES,
2001c). Little emphasis is given to the need for global co-operation.

Young people are expected to 'take increasing responsibility for
their own learning' (*ibid.*, 18. 3.2). This would seem to imply processes of democratisation in schools, but in contrast to the situation
in many other European countries, education legislation in England
does not guarantee student representation in school decision-
making (Davies and Kirkpatrick, 2000; Osler and Vincent, 2002).
Thus, the accountability of schools and education authorities does
not appear to extend to learners. Schools are required to improve
standards so that students will be well placed to make their contribution to an internationally competitive workforce. Globalisation is
seen largely as an economic process and not as a potential force for
greater democratisation and one which will require all citizens to
develop skills for living together peaceably. Consequently, education

policy does not prioritise this issue or give particular emphasis to the development of democratic skills (Osler and Vincent, 2002). Nevertheless, the introduction of citizenship education as part of the national curriculum for England from 2002 provides one means by which students might be given the opportunity to develop such skills.

We argue that policies for social inclusion need to acknowledge processes of globalisation. Globalisation does not merely imply a set of economic processes but the development of democratic institutions and processes at all levels in order to influence the future world in which we live. The processes of globalisation and democratisation demand education for peace, democracy and human rights and the development of a global ethic (Osler and Starkey, 1996 and 2001a; Osler and Vincent, 2002). We have argued that schools will need to prepare learners for global citizenship as well as enabling them to develop the skills and attitudes necessary for living together in local communities and states which are increasingly diverse in their make-up. We refer to this as education for cosmopolitan citizenship. Among the qualities of an educated cosmopolitan citizen are: skills to cope with change and uncertainty; respect for diversity between people, according to gender, ethnicity and culture; recognition that their own worldview is shaped by personal and societal history and by cultural tradition; and solidarity with and compassion for others (UNESCO, 1995a). The development of these skills and attitudes for living together is an essential feature of education, as important to all citizens as basic literacy and numeracy, and critical in the development of our vision of a future successful multicultural society (Osler,1999b; Osler and Starkey, 2000a; Parekh, 2000).

This vision of an inclusionary curriculum is at odds with the statutory framework in which schools in England are required to operate. From the early years of schooling young people (and their teachers) are subject to a long process of preparing and sitting for a series of national tests. Tests do serve the function of informing us how successful schools are in meeting the needs of different groupings of students, providing us with information which can then be used to re-direct resources to meet the needs of those who need additional support. However, the government sees schools as having failed their students and the tests are first and foremost a means by which schools can be held accountable to parents. The testing regime is one means by which the 'failure' of the school system can be addressed. A key government education adviser argues that what is required is:

> urgent reform of the basic school system. Like the US, [Britain] has an internationally renowned university sector with impressive rates of graduation and post-graduate study. But these co-exist with a school system, which, historically, has failed the majority. Tackling this basic failure – in the light of the rapidly escalating requirements of the new economy – makes education such a central political priority for Britain's Labour Party.
>
> (Adonis, 2001: 6)

A number of researchers examining, in particular, government discourses and administrative frameworks relating to the education of students with special needs have noted the tensions and contractions between the stated commitment to inclusion and the quasi-market which operates. In this system considerable emphasis is placed on attainment targets and testing, and parents are seen as citizen-consumers selecting the schools with the best results. Students who appear likely to do well in examinations are favoured over others who may require more support and more resources. Researchers examining the impact since 1997 of the Labour government's education policy, which is based on notions of 'stakeholder welfare', have identified what they refer to as 'incremental dissonance'. They argue that 'the layering of new policies that have as their notional objective "inclusion" on top of practices that have demonstrably contrary effects' serve to prevent inclusionary outcomes for children and young people who, for various reasons, fail to perform in this market (Loxley and Thomas, 2001: 299). They argue that dissonance has occurred because the policies have been introduced without addressing the overall legislative framework in education, introduced by the Thatcher government from the late 1980s, which was informed by a belief in the importance of individualism and the free market.

It has been argued that the cycles of preparation and assessment in operation in English schools are more intrusive than in many other countries (Jeffs, 2002). Although a number of researchers and the teacher unions have argued that these assessment processes have had a significant and negative impact on both teacher morale and professionalism, our own research suggests a more complex picture.

Data collected in the mid-1990s as part of a life history project with British teachers from black and Asian communities, revealed that, despite concerns about exclusionary practices, the majority had managed to maintain some of the idealism with which they had entered teaching and that a number, particularly those in senior positions, held a vision of the potential transformatory power of education (Osler, 1997c). Further research with (mostly white) headteachers, carried out in 2000, just a year after the publication of the Stephen Lawrence Inquiry report, revealed that they were generally ready and willing to develop a more inclusive curriculum and more inclusive schools. They recognised the importance of preparing all students to respond positively to diversity and to promote justice and equality. However, most felt they needed specialised guidance and training (Osler and Morrison, 2000). Most importantly, they noted the lack of both political and institutional leadership in this area:

> They had been moved by the findings of the Stephen Lawrence inquiry which highlighted the institutionalised nature of racism, not only within the police force but also across all the institutions of society. Yet, they were not convinced that race equality in education is a genuine government priority or confident that OFSTED inspectors have the necessary expertise to inspect this area. As one secondary headteacher expressed it: 'If race equality is a government priority in education no one has made it clear to me'.
>
> (Osler and Morrison, 2002: 334)

The evidence suggests that despite problems with teacher morale and retention many teachers and school leaders still maintain a strong commitment to social justice and inclusion. The importance of political and institutional leadership in the development of genuinely inclusive schools which prepare all students to participate as members of a new multicultural society in which they feel they have a role to play cannot be over-stated. Yet it is insufficient to hope that one particular curriculum subject, such as Citizenship, can achieve this goal unless real changes are brought about in teachers' working lives and the stated and actual priorities of both initial teacher education and programmes for teachers' continuing professional development. As part of a project setting out to identify the steps necessary to realise Britain as a new inclusive multicultural society, a number of white British teachers were invited to talk about their professional roles and responsibilities in relation to the development of our future society and globalised world:

> Only one teacher had given this any thought. The rest were consumed with tests, the league tables, and big bad inspectors. It felt like I was interviewing a passport official about our immigration policies. Their worlds were so officiated that they could not see beyond them at all.
>
> (Alibhai-Brown, 2001: 175–6)

The pressures of teachers' everyday responsibilities have led many to focus on the minutiae of their working lives as they struggle to survive. But this is not to place blame on teachers or to argue that all that is required is a change of perspective. Many of the problems are systemic. Pressures on schools to 'raise standards' within a context where academic results are published in annual league tables have led them instead to compete for students. Rather than raise standards by addressing the needs of those who are educationally disadvantaged (and thus relatively expensive to educate) schools compete for high-attaining students who can succeed with fewer resources. In this context, education for living together takes second place to schooling which ensures that the maximum numbers of students achieve good grades in public examinations. There would seem to be no reason why enabling all students to achieve their maximum potential cannot be compatible with and even contribute to the goals of social cohesion and inclusion. Yet within the quasi-market system in operation, producing such tensions between 'standards' and inclusion, these goals tend to be seen as an after-thought.

The problem of rationing education (Gillborn and Youdell, 2000) appears to have been most acutely experienced within the particular quasi-market system operating in England, but is not peculiar to this context. An organisation providing New Zealand parents with legal advice on matters relating to schooling, reports that the four key areas of parental concern relate to suspensions and exclusions; special needs, school fees and inappropriate discipline. Schools argue that the Special Education Grant (SEG) is inadequate to meet the needs of all students with special needs in this category and there are a number of cases of discrimination against them. The Wellington Community Law Centre notes that some schools are clearly excluding children as they prioritise the needs of academically successful students over those who are judged to have mild to moderate special educational needs:

> Schools, both principals and boards, often seem to ask themselves 'what do we need to do to get rid of x without legal ramifications' rather than 'what measures do we need to implement to be able to meet x's needs at this school?'
> Unfortunately some schools seem to place more emphasis on assisting students with potential for excellence, rather than helping students with special needs reach their full potential.
> (Darlow, 2001: 17)

Market forces have had a direct impact on both formal and informal exclusions, truancy levels and drop-out rates in England, with 'successful' schools able to reject, neglect or simply lose those students whose education is resource intensive (Hayden, 1997; Osler and Osler, 2002). Some young people may effectively be excluded from the school culture before they experience disciplinary exclusion (Pomeroy, 2000). Some schools are able to demonstrate low formal exclusion rates while at the same time engaging in practices which serve to exclude and alienate many students: 'the absence of formal exclusion does not automatically imply the presence of inclusion' (Cooper et al., 2000: 9).

Gender, ethnicity and exclusion

We have seen in chapter 1 how exclusion from school is linked, in media discourses, to concerns about (male) youth violence, even though relatively few students are excluded from school for violent behaviour. This chapter has highlighted how the British government, which originally identified exclusion from school as a sanction which schools were using too freely, has shifted the terms of the debate. Exclusion from school is no longer presented as something likely to lead to longer-term social exclusion but as a reasonable response to bad behaviour which, if not addressed in this way, would be likely to undermine the drive to improve 'standards'. We have also shown how most attention has focused on boys, who are, at the peak age for exclusion, in the final years of secondary school, three times more likely than girls to experience permanent exclusion as a disciplinary measure. When exclusion statistics peaked during the mid-1990s, black boys were six times more likely to be excluded from school than white boys. Black girls were also much more vulnerable to exclusion than their white female peers, with national statistics suggesting that they were eight times more likely to be excluded (Osler and Hill, 1999). Although the government set targets to reduce the number of exclusions by one-third, no targets were set to address either the disproportionate number of boys formally excluded or the disproportionate number of black students formally excluded. Differential rates of suspension and exclusion between different ethnic groups are not peculiar to England. In New Zealand, for example, the suspension rate for Pakeha (white) students is 10.9 per 1000, compared with 35.8 per 1000 for Maori students and 19.3 per 1000 for Pacific students (Alton-Lee and Praat, 2001).

Our research, presented in the following chapters, shows that although reduction targets in England were not gender specific, responses to exclusion have largely focused on boys. The media have been less likely to highlight the over-representation of black students within exclusion statistics, but when this issue has been raised, the focus again has been on boys rather than on girls. Drawing on our own earlier research findings and on those of others, we have argued strongly for government and local education authorities to give strong leadership in addressing racial inequalities in the use of exclusion:

> All the evidence suggests that if schools are able to access appropriate support from a range of agencies, the rise in the level of exclusions can be reversed; the government's decision to set targets to achieve this is to be welcomed. It is critical, however, if we are to ensure racial equality in this aspect of education policy, that specific targets are set to reduce the current over-representation of African-Caribbean pupils in the exclusion statistics and to end racial inequalities, within a fixed time period. Such target setting is critical in addressing current inequalities in outcomes. Our research demonstrates that schools which adopt a 'colour blind' approach to the reduction of school exclusions are successful in cutting exclusion for all groups, but do not address existing inequalities, leaving particular ethnic groups vulnerable to exclusion. Schools and LEAs are more likely to find effective and creative solutions to reduce black over-representation if central government demonstrates that it sees this as a priority.
>
> (Osler and Hill, 1999: 60)

It is curious that, although there has been a moral panic over boys' 'underachievement' and exclusion, very little media or political attention has been given to the racial equalities in exclusion rates and attainment. The government's reluctance to set targets in this area, in the face of evidence of gross racial inequalities, suggests that the notion of social justice and inclusion promoted in the 1998 SEU report on school exclusions was somewhat incomplete. The accepted wisdom among education professionals is, however, that black boys are likely to be excluded, but that black girls are doing very well. Consequently, black girls' particular vulnerability to disciplinary exclusion is simply overlooked. Policies which address social inclusion and school inclusion are relatively meaningless unless this systemic discrimination within education is addressed. The Race Relations (Amendment) Act 2000 requires public bodies, including schools and LEAs, not only to prevent discrimination but to promote race equality. Specifically, schools and LEAs have a statutory duty to provide a race impact assessment of their policies and their effect on attainment levels. This requires them to consider the impact of policies on the number of disciplinary exclusions. Yet the initial response when this legislation came into effect in May 2002 was somewhat mixed, with National Association of Headteachers (NAHT) leader David Hart complaining about members' workloads and lack of preparation time.

Teacher expectations have been highlighted as a key issue in understanding inequalities in the treatment of minority students, but this is an area which education ministers have been reluctant to address, preferring to focus instead on questions of student behaviour. Perhaps this is because, as Maud Blair asserts, 'Racism is a particularly touchy subject for many teachers' (2001: 58) and certainly for a number of the teacher unions. Yet our research shows that teachers may adopt 'racial frames of reference' (Figueroa, 1991) in dealing with black students and that these frames of reference are likely to be gender specific. As one experienced primary teacher explained:

> The over-representation of African-Caribbean boys [among those excluded] is a very complicated issue, but I think expectations make a big difference, and I think we do tend, however well intentioned, to see a black boy and think they are going to be trouble. A lot of this is down to the curriculum. I think that one of the problems is that after a long period of dependency

> [on National Curriculum requirements] and I'm thinking of
> new teachers now, there is a whole generation of teachers who
> came in to schools without the grounding of making decisions
> about what is appropriate.
>
> (quoted in Osler and Hill, 1999: 47)

Not only is this teacher acknowledging the ways in which teachers
operate within racial and gendered frames of reference, but she is
arguing that, since the late 1980s teachers have not been trained to
engage in curriculum development. Consequently, although originally tight National Curriculum guidelines have been revised, allowing for increasing flexibility, many teachers are unprepared and
inexperienced in selecting materials which are inclusive of all students. Although the most recent guidelines stress the importance of
inclusivity, and the importance of recognising and accepting diversity, there has been limited public debate about the role of education
in countering racism and other anti-democratic forces through education (Osler and Starkey, 2002a). Education ministers have been
slow to take a lead in this field. Following the Stephen Lawrence
inquiry report (Macpherson, 1999), when senior government figures
acknowledged institutional racism across British society, no education minister has ever acknowledged institutional racism within the
education service (Osler, 2002). Consequently, it is easier to recognise racism as something which occurs between students rather than
something which is embedded in the education service and in which
teachers may be implicated. Unless we are able to develop a climate
in which teachers are able to discuss these questions openly, it is
unlikely we will be able to develop strategies to tackle inequalities
and ensure inclusive schools.

Excluding girls

The research on which we focus in this book not only examines the
ways in which schools operate to exclude girls, but drawing on girls'
own accounts, and on those of a range of professionals who work
with them, explores how girls respond to school, and how they self-
exclude and withdraw from learning. The girls in this study also
spoke to us about bullying and described the exclusionary practices
which girls may adopt towards each other. They spoke of the support and fun which friendship offered but also of stress and conflict.
They suggested that friendships were much more important to girls

than to boys and that when thing went wrong it was far more difficult for girls to make up than it was for boys. These girls argued that bullying between girls often led to various forms of exclusion. They demonstrated how bullying between girls is often 'subtle' in nature and not easily recognised by teachers. Girls who decide to stand up to bullies, or who suffer in silence and finally lash out, may find themselves subject to disciplinary exclusion. Alternatively those who experience bullying might self-exclude by truanting or by withdrawing from active participation in school.

Friendships and girls' own exclusionary practices both clearly have a direct impact on the ways in which girls experience school. Hey (1997: 129) asserts that 'understanding girls' intimate friendship demands paradoxically that we have to understand the social force of hegemonic masculinity'. Girls placed a great deal of store on 'reputation' and on being liked by others. This requires girls to position themselves carefully within a heterosexual hegemony, to ensure that they are friendly and attractive to boys. Girls whose identities do not include being heterosexual may experience difficulties in understanding their own feelings, isolation and stress within schools which fail to acknowledge other identities (Vincent and Ballard, 1997); such experiences are likely to be exclusionary in outcome. The girls in our study reported how the maintenance of 'reputation' involved establishing a clear heterosexual identity and showing an interest in boys; it was important to be friendly to other girls and boys but to avoid any suggestion of lesbianism. On the other hand, girls had to tread a fine line between being seen as interested in and attractive to boys and avoiding damage to their reputation by being labelled as promiscuous; a girl who was accused of sleeping around was likely to be ostracised. Girls used friendship and the withholding of friendship and the inclusion or exclusion of other girls from friendship groups as a means of exercising power and control over each other.

Both black and white girls may find themselves subject to similar controls by their peers. In the case of black girls the forms of exclusion may be further complicated by elements of racial harassment and by differential responses from teachers, operating within racial frames of reference. Blair (2001) provides an illustration of this in this quote by Glenda, a 15-year-old black student, who describes what happened to her and her two friends. Glenda stresses the importance of friendship to girls and illustrates how teachers' actions may have unintended but nevertheless discriminatory and exclusionary outcomes:

> [T]his group of white girls started calling us names, racial names and calling us slags, and so we started calling them names. Anyway, it got really bad and Mr Martin, the Deputy Head decided it had to end. So he calls us three black girls and tells us that he never wants to see us together in the playground again, and so every break, Isobel has to go to that corner of the playground, (pointing) I have to go to that one, and Lorene has to go to that one. But the white girls can stay as friends and don't have to split up. And now Isobel hardly ever comes to school and me and Lorene sometimes bunk off because there's just no point coming to school if you can't be with your friends.
>
> (Blair, 2001: 78)

Official attention on those who are subject to disciplinary exclusion has led to neglect of other forms of exclusion. Through the accounts of girls and the professionals who work with them we examine some of the barriers to girls' achievement and inclusion, including limited access to educational alternatives, such as places in special schools for students with emotional and behavioural difficulties. Other barriers to success and participation in school include parentally condoned absences, low aspirations, caring responsibilities and sexual exploitation. We suggest that some of these problems are more likely to be overlooked by teachers when they are considering female, rather than male, students. Many of these concerns manifest themselves in non-attendance and the issue of self-exclusion and opting out was identified as a particular problem among such girls. The government recognises the problem of 'truancy', but tactics such as 'sweeps' of shopping malls to pick up truants are unlikely to address the complex underlying causes of the phenomena of non-attendance.

Girls are also vulnerable to exclusion as a result of the ways in which their problems are categorised and measured and resources allocated. For example, suicide rates for girls and young women are relatively low, compared with those for boys. In 1996 the UK rate was four per 100,000, giving a total of 154 young women who died through suicide (Dennison and Coleman, 2000). However, if the problem is re-conceptualised to acknowledge the variation in suicide rates between different ethnic groups and to address the widespread problem of self-harm among young women, the picture looks quite different. Adolescent boys are more likely to commit suicide but girls and young women to attempt it. Three times more young women than young men engage in self-harming behaviour and the group most likely to engage in such behaviour are girls aged 13–15 years (Meltzer *et al.*, 2001). The researchers report that while rates of mental health problems are higher for boys, rates of emotional disorder are higher in girls. Young women are twice as likely to suffer a depressive disorder (Dennison and Coleman, 2000). In New Zealand a similar pattern emerges. Boys are more likely than girls to commit suicide, but girls more likely to attempt it. Girls are also known to experience higher rates of depression and anxiety disorders than boys. Young Maori men and women are more likely to commit suicide than their non-Maori counterparts (Alton-Lee and Praat, 2001). If we are to understand the multiple and complex ways in which exclusion occurs, we need to acknowledge and examine the ways in which we conceptualise problems, ensuring that girls' as well as boys' needs are addressed and recognising that within the overall categories 'girls' and 'boys' there are further groupings of young people with specific needs.

In seeking to understand the ways in which girls experience exclusion from school, we argue that it is essential to question the ways in which problems have been conceptualised. We also need to broaden our understandings of exclusion to cover unofficial as well as official disciplinary exclusions, self-exclusion and withdrawal from learning and participation in the school community. In other words, our definition of exclusion needs to address all those young people who are effectively excluded from the processes of learning, even though some of them may be in school or recorded as being in school. It is also important, when considering the specific needs of girls and young women, to keep in mind other factors such as ethnicity, age and special educational needs. Exclusion and inclusion should be seen as part of a continuum, with individuals moving along that continuum at different points in their school careers.

Part II

Girls in and out of school

Chapter 3

Sanctions and support

In this chapter we focus on the services, sanctions and support which are targeted at disaffected youth. Drawing on girls' own accounts as well as those of various professionals who work with them, we examine the relationship between the different conceptualisations of girls' and boys' problems and the ways in which resources are allocated and accessed by different groups of young people.

Our study into girls and exclusion from school set out to increase understanding of the forms and causes of exclusion from school, as experienced by girls, and to enable the development of more effective support strategies for girls. In part 1 of this book we demonstrated how the scale of the problem has been underestimated, showing how a focus on permanent disciplinary exclusions masks other forms of exclusion which can have equally devastating effects on girls' lives. We examined how girls have been presented as successful in comparison to boys, and how media discourses which focus on (male) youth disaffection and on a 'crisis of masculinity' have served to render girls and young women invisible. We showed how the good intentions of government to tackle school exclusion as a cause of social exclusion have been undermined. Government ministers, teacher unions and the media have increasingly presented young people as a problem. They present youth as ill-disciplined, a threat to teachers and to the government's programme of improving standards. We have argued that such discourses marginalise young people in general and girls in particular. The young, who lack political power and who are regularly denied participation rights in education, are presented as the prime cause of what are, in reality, complex problems with complex causes. We have argued that there needs to be a renewed effort to address school exclusion and to

challenge institutional cultures of exclusion. This requires a re-
definition of exclusion and inclusion, taking into account the needs
and experiences of girls as well as those of boys.

In order to understand the processes by which young people are
subject to various sanctions and the ways in which they access support, we talked to girls themselves and to service providers about
girls' experiences in school and in alternative educational provision.
We asked them to consider whether and how these experiences dif-
fer from those of boys and how, when difficulties arise, girls access
support. We reflect further on the questions raised in chapter 1
about the ways in which 'problem behaviour' is conceptualised in
relation to girls and the ways in which dominant discourses about
masculinity and femininity may impact on girls. We draw on these
discourses in order to understand the processes through which particular types of need are identified, and support is offered and
accessed. In particular, we draw on girls' own perceptions of the
ways in which they conduct themselves in school and the ways in
which they interpret and respond to teachers' behaviour, in order to
analyse these processes. We compare and contrast these young
women's perceptions with those of a range of professionals. We
contend that how we think about what it is to be male or female has
a real impact not only on the ways in which we conceptualise and
respond to 'problem behaviour' and identify those in need but also
on the ways in which service providers allocate resources.

Girls' exclusion in England: constructing a national picture

Nationally, our knowledge about both the number and characteristics of pupils who are disaffected or who experience exclusionary
sanctions remains limited. We have seen how girls make up one in
four of those students who are permanently excluded as a disciplinary measure in the latter years of secondary school. The Department for Education and Skills provides an annual statistical report
which includes a statistical breakdown by gender and by ethnicity.
Unfortunately, these variables were not put together to allow an
analysis of gender alongside ethnicity.[1] Consequently, there has
been, to date, no national mapping of which girls or which boys are
most vulnerable to exclusion. We are therefore dependent on
smaller studies and on secondary analysis of national data to reveal,
for example, that black girls are particularly vulnerable to exclusion,

compared with their female peers (Osler and Hill, 1999). Our research on girls and the various ways in which they experience exclusion is therefore set within a national picture which is somewhat incomplete. Those pieces of the jigsaw which we have relate largely to formal permanent disciplinary exclusions, which are a small proportion of the total, and to boys, who make up the majority of students subject to this form of exclusion and about whom most has been written. Yet, national policies and local practices have been developed from this limited knowledge base.

We have already noted how permanent disciplinary exclusions form a small proportion of the total number. There are currently no national figures for fixed-period exclusions or the proportion of this total that is girls. Annual numbers of fixed-term exclusions are estimated to be more than 10 times higher than the number of officially recorded permanent exclusions (Audit Commission, 1999). While there is growing evidence of various forms of informal exclusion (Lloyd, 2000; Osler *et al.*, 2000), little is known about the extent of such practices or about which groups may be most vulnerable to them. The use of internal exclusion (removal of a pupil from classes) appears to be an accepted disciplinary practice in some schools. It is applied in an informal way. This means that systematic records are rarely kept. Consequently, little is known about the extent of these exclusions or whether they are disproportionately used against girls or boys.

DfES statistics (2001d) show that secondary schools report losing around 1.1 per cent of school time to unauthorised absence. There is some evidence that official figures significantly under-represent the magnitude of the problem. The results of anonymised surveys of pupils suggest that actual levels of truancy are far higher than the official figures indicate (Social Exclusion Unit, 1998; Reid, 1999). Within the sample of girls interviewed for this study, all but one admitted to skipping a lesson on at least one occasion. Official figures do not include post-registration truancy, yet the girls also pointed out how, in most schools, it is possible to register and then quietly disappear.

Although the Social Exclusion Unit (1998) reports that truancy rates among boys and girls appear to be similar, it is not clear what the basis for this assertion is. In fact, local education authorities have never been asked to provide a gender breakdown of truancy statistics. The results of surveys which suggest similar levels of truancy between the sexes need cautious interpretation. Reid (1999) found that girls are two to three times more likely to be involved in parentally condoned unauthorised absences than are boys, yet some studies do not classify parentally condoned absences as truancy. It is likely, therefore, that girls' levels of truancy may be significantly underestimated.

Thus, the true extent of unauthorised absence and the number and characteristics of students who experience fixed-period, internal and informal exclusion remain unclear. We set out to discover more about the types of support available to students judged to be disaffected. In particular, we wished to establish the degree to which such support is available to girls, which girls are accessing it, and whether or not it meets their needs. This information is critical for the assessment and development of current support practices and for the future targeting of resources.

Policy and provision for disaffected and excluded pupils

From 1999, the government made available nearly £500 million over three years to assist schools in tackling behaviour problems and disaffection. One key mechanism was the Social Inclusion Pupil Support Grant, which was intended to support programmes to reduce non-attendance and disruptive behaviour within schools, and which was made available through local education authorities (LEAs). Schools have also been able to access funds directly through the mainstream Standards Fund and through particular initiatives targeted at schools in the most disadvantaged areas, such as Excellence in Cities and education action zones.

Schools and LEAs are subject to detailed statutory guidance on student behaviour and support in order to enable social inclusion, and have been issued with specific advice concerning truancy (DfEE, 1999a, b and c). Such guidance covers attendance, alternative provision and students who are excluded or at risk of exclusion. Specific strategies advocated include mentoring, the development of individual behaviour support plans, work-related learning, in-school centres, pupil referral units, and the use of further education colleges for under-16-year-olds and individual and home tuition. Not only the Department for Education and Skills but other ministries have been active in developing initiatives aimed at promoting social inclusion.[2] Central government advocates LEA partnerships with voluntary organisations:

Contractual arrangements with voluntary organisations can be an effective way for LEAs to meet their duty to provide education out of school. LEAs can place pupils in units run by voluntary bodies that provide education and training for disaffected young people.

(DfEE, 1999b: 5.17)

The various government funding mechanisms seek to promote multi-agency approaches in supporting vulnerable young people.[3] At the time of our research in 2000/2001 many of the initiatives we examined were at an early stage. Nevertheless, it was clear that multi-agency approaches were being developed.

Unequal access

Previous research examining special educational needs (SEN) provision available in England confirms that 'there has been a marked disparity of provision for boys and girls in access to many special schools' (Daniels et al., 1999: 190). The researchers found that in mainstream schools not only were significantly more boys than girls allocated such support but also that these boys received more hours of support and more expensive forms of support than their female classmates. The most marked gender differences occurred among those students who were classified as having emotional and behavioural difficulties (EBD).

An earlier study of girls' experiences of disruption in a mixed urban comprehensive school also revealed gross disparities in terms of resources allocated to managing the behaviour of boys and girls. These disparities were experienced in terms of referrals to internal school support systems, the LEA specialist behavioural support team and educational psychologists. The authors concluded that 'It was hard to believe that girls were five times less likely than boys to need attention for reasons to do with their behaviour' (Crozier and Anstiss, 1995: 35). Not only were boys more likely to be referred to such agencies, they were also much more likely to experience fixed-term exclusions from the school. Girls themselves were aware of the imbalances in the amount of attention given to boys and girls. They expressed their sense of injustice through comments such as ' "It's their school" and "they can do what they like" ' (Crozier and Anstiss, 1995: 43). Within our study, a visit to an in-school support centre revealed a similar imbalance between boys and girls.[4]

Service providers interviewed as part of our study also believe that there is a gender bias in the way resources are allocated to support disaffected pupils:

> There is quite a male predominance in the youngsters we were looking at where schools have made alternative arrangements. They were nearly all for male pupils.
>
> (educational welfare officer)

Our own analysis of data provided by two LEAs confirms the perceptions of these professionals working with young people. Out of a total of 1,740 students accessing the alternative education schemes we surveyed which were open to both sexes, just 25 per cent (433) were girls. Boys were accessing a disproportionate number of places in pastoral support, behavioural support and other alternative education schemes. Special projects run by voluntary organisations were least likely to include girls. Just 27 per cent of under-16-year-olds attending further education colleges as an alternative to school were girls. The ratio of boys to girls attending such provision (3:1) is equivalent to that of boys and girls permanently excluded from school. Yet we know that a significant number of the girls in the alternative provision were there for reasons other than disciplinary exclusion. For example, some had stopped attending their mainstream school and others were pregnant.

In one of the LEAs, a multi-agency panel made decisions and arrangements for those needing alternative education. Pupils referred included excluded pupils, truants, school phobics, pregnant schoolgirls and those with long-term medical conditions. This panel allocated placements to LEA-run services such as the pupil referral unit but also to a number of charitable trusts who ran programmes for excluded or disaffected young people. The LEA offered a range of full-time and part-time courses at the local further education college, and an under-16s co-ordinator was employed there. Figures for 1999/2000 indicated that out of 160 referrals, just 55 (34 per cent) were girls. The LEA official who provided these statistics indicated that this percentage would be much lower if pregnant schoolgirls and those with a long-term illness or attendance difficulties were not included.[5]

A project worker on a Home Office-funded initiative explained that although both boys and girls were eligible for this alternative education programme most participants had been male. This

interviewee explained that the two girls who had accessed the programme that year had 'pulled out because they didn't want to mix
with the lads', suggesting that for many girls being in a largely male
environment can be problematic. Home Office projects target those
who are at risk of involvement in criminal activities as well as those
who are disaffected or excluded from school. As young women are
statistically less likely to be involved in crime than young men, it is
likely that their referral rates will be lower.

School cultures and gendered perceptions of behaviour

We have seen how support and access to alternative educational
opportunities are most commonly realised as a result of professional referral, following concerns about an individual's behaviour
or ability to cope within the mainstream school environment. We
now consider why more boys than girls are subject to disciplinary
sanctions and targeted for support. We illustrate how professionals
recognise a complex range of needs, which tend to be expressed in
different ways by boys and girls. However, they commonly argue
that access to support is more likely to be triggered by a school's
need to deal with an acute behaviour problem which is hindering the
day-to-day business of the school and teachers' work rather than a
complex and rounded assessment of a student's social, emotional
and learning needs.

The view that two different students can behave in more or less
the same way but that the behaviour is perceived differently according to whether the student is male or female was expressed by a
number of service providers and also by some parents. It was argued
that girls are sometimes given more leeway than are boys in relation
to aggressive behaviour. Whereas a certain degree of aggression in
boys is accepted as 'natural', if it is not checked it becomes threatening and must be brought under control. Thus a boy displaying
aggressive behaviour might need to be punished. However, aggression in girls is not normally seen as 'natural' and may be seen as
representing a more deep-seated problem for which she requires
help:

> I think there is an assumption that if a female is showing aggres-
> sive behaviours, it doesn't really fit in with the stereotype, so
> they think there must really be something wrong here . . . let's

just try and sort it out. But if a boy does the same thing then that's it, they're out.

(educational psychologist)

Alternatively, girls who behave aggressively may be judged as out-rageous or extreme and therefore liable to experience more severe punishments than boys:

Girls are greater victims of inconsistencies; there is a degree of intolerance but also a degree of shock and horror: they do not have the ability to be 'loveable rogues'.

(head of pupil referral unit (PRU))

Girls also identified gender-based differences in treatment by some teachers. Although they thought that greater leniency might be shown to either boys or girls depending on the teacher involved, the comment from the student below also suggests that certain behaviours that are seen to be atypical of girls may attract teacher attention. The student suggests that the same behaviour in boys is more likely to be tolerated:

Some teachers like the girls more than the boys or the boys more than the girls. And the girls or boys will get away with things. And sometimes the teacher will say 'Oh, I know that he usually does that' so they just let it go and leave it, but if a girl does it they say, 'That's not like you, why did you do that?'

(Kim, mainstream school, no exclusions)

Both the girls' and service providers' views echo other recent research that suggests that girls who behave in ways that run counter to traditional forms of femininity are labelled more negatively than boys who behave in similar ways (Reay, 2001). While we do not know the relationship between such labelling and girls' likelihood of experiencing disciplinary sanctions, or alternatively, accessing additional support, it is clear that girls themselves do perceive such inconsistencies to occur. This, in turn, is likely to affect how they respond to teachers and manage particular encounters.

Certainly, some professionals perceive school cultures to be more girl-friendly than boy-friendly. Drawing on current discourses about boys' 'underachievement' and a crisis of masculinity,[6] they explain boys' failure in terms of teaching methods, the nature of academic work and the fact that a large part of the school day involves long periods of sitting and concentrating. These factors are used by these professionals to explain why boys are underachieving and/or being subject to formal disciplinary exclusion in larger numbers:

> I think that there is definitely something to do with boys being less suited to the culture of schools than girls . . . that schools are more friendly places for girls. And I think that some of that is to do with quite early stuff . . . literacy and the acquisition of language . . . that girls start the educational process that little bit more advanced than boys.
>
> (deputy headteacher, mainstream school)

A few interviewees suggested that schooling, which involves long periods of concentration, favours girls. They argued for a greater emphasis on competition and on approaches which focus on outcomes rather than processes, believing that such methods will favour boys. In presenting such viewpoints, none of these professionals acknowledged or explained why a significant minority of boys (44 per cent) continue to flourish and succeed, achieving top grades under current, supposedly girl-friendly arrangements. Nor did they explain why apparently girl-friendly methods still allow a substantial minority of girls (around 45 per cent) to leave school without having achieved good grades. As discussed in chapter 1, these professionals seem to reflect public and media discourses which see girls as succeeding *at the expense of boys*. In this apparent competition between the sexes, they advocate methods which will redress the balance by disadvantaging girls, rather than consider how all students can be encouraged to achieve.

Managing teachers and school

Interviewees, both girls and service providers, perceived girls as more mature but also more socially aware and more intentional in their actions, both with regard to getting into trouble and getting out of trouble. For example, girls were seen as more likely to use apologies strategically:

> Part of the reason girls don't get excluded as much is because

they are better at social skills. When they do get into bother, they are much better at dropping the eyes and saying I'm sorry.

(member of behaviour support service)

Anna, a Year 11 student, agreed:

Girls apologise . . . and well, they can act innocent. They just, when they put a foot wrong, well they're just like 'Oh I'm sorry I didn't mean to do it, I'll never do it again', but with boys they're just like 'Yeah so what?'

(permanently excluded student, attending PRU)

Anna went on to suggest that apologising is less frequently used by boys because they want to 'look hard' in front of their friends, implying cultural pressures on boys to behave in ways that may make them more vulnerable to school disciplinary procedures.

Other girls also referred to the use of verbal communication skills such as 'making excuses' and 'talking your way out of it' as ways in which girls negotiated their way out of trouble:

Girls, they can talk their way out of some things . . . like they make excuses for themselves. And boys, when they get into trouble, they just make it worse by like shouting at the teacher and denying what they've done.

(Nicole, mainstream school, no exclusions)

Crying was another tactic identified by the girls:

And more girls seem to cry when the teacher tells them off . . . I've done that and it's worked.

(Louise, mainstream school, fixed-term
and permanent exclusions)

When asked what effect crying might have on teachers another interviewee explained: 'They've got softer hearts' (Nadine, PRU, fixed-term and permanent exclusions).

Some service providers thought that girls are generally more likely to consider the consequences of their actions and to modify their actions accordingly. This might involve, for example, predicting a particular teacher's likely response to language that falls outside the acceptable norm in schools. As one educational psychologist put it:

'If you say "fuck off" to the newly qualified French teacher then you might get away with it, but if you say it to the head of year then you're out'.

In line with this, girls tended to view some boys' behaviour as 'stupid' when they perceived them as acting without thinking through the consequences. Girls in one group interview explained that 'arguing a mature point in class' was more likely to get a better teacher response and lead to the desired outcome than a less considered reaction.

S1: I think some of these boys are just so stupid they don't stop to think 'Well, wait a minute, if I argue it in this way, I could get away with it'.

S2: Exactly . . . like Tony, he just screams. I mean, you can't really do that 'cause then they [teachers] can have a go at you. If you argue a mature point in class, they'll talk to you maturely afterwards and that's when you get to say, 'Yes, but I really didn't blah, blah'.

(speakers in group interview, mainstream school)

Girls were also perceived by a range of service providers as being less direct in their challenges to authority and more covert when engaging in disruptive behaviour. A hushed comment that results in a wave of giggling may undermine a teacher's authority just as effectively as an audible inappropriate remark or a direct refusal to comply with a request. The former, however, is somewhat more difficult for the teacher to respond to. Girls are not necessarily passively compliant and accepting of school requirements, but instead have been found to actively and flexibly deploy a range of strategies to manage their schooling experiences (Whitelaw et al., 2000).

Coping strategies and peer pressures

The vast majority of the professionals argued that girls and boys generally have the same or similar needs at school. However, they felt that when needs are not being adequately met, girls are likely to employ different strategies from boys in order to manage the situation.

Boys will present as aggressive and violent when they are having problems, so they are immediately identified in the school setting. Girls don't. Girls tend to become withdrawn and they will use their friends . . . cry a lot . . . and withdraw from school.

(education welfare officer)

Girls are generally viewed as quieter, more compliant, less physical and more likely to support each other. Consequently, they may withdraw and either absent themselves from school or engage in behaviours which, although damaging, are not necessarily likely to attract the attention of teachers:

I think girls tend to internalise things more and to self-exclude . . . stay in bed. Or they'll self harm or develop some sort of eating disorder . . . those sorts of things. Boys are more likely to express their anger externally and that's probably where they get exclusions happening.

(children's rights officer)

Boys, on the other hand, are seen as generally louder, more physical and more likely to 'act out' in ways that require an immediate response from the teacher:

Boys that don't cope with the curriculum act out. Girls withdraw, physically and emotionally . . . and also, girls are quieter on the whole.

(headteacher, PRU)

These professionals' observations confirm research findings which indicate that more girls than boys are at risk of internalising disorders such as anxiety and depression and that among girls there is a higher incidence of suicide attempts and other self-harming behaviours (Keenan et al., 1999; Dennison and Coleman, 2000).

Within the community of a school, a covert or internalised response such as withdrawal may appear more socially acceptable than angry or aggressive behaviour which disrupts everyone's learning. Such responses are not necessarily less disruptive to the individual's own learning. Certain behaviours, such as cutting or forms of self-harm, can be hidden from adults who would find them socially unacceptable or see them as a cry for help. As a recent report notes:

[The cutters] are usually but not always girls, and aged between

13 and 15. Very often their parents have no idea what they are doing, nor do their teachers. Their peers do not seem to see the self-abuse as profoundly disturbing, more as something that is 'stupid', 'ignorant' and 'sad' in the sense of pathetic.

(Gerrard, 2002: 16)

The coping strategies typical of girls that enable them to avoid getting into trouble also prevent them from accessing sources of support. Thus, girls' typical management strategies, whether they involve internalising stress or self-excluding, bring their own negative consequences. Friends may be able to listen and support each other, but be ill-informed about longer-term sources of help. Covert responses to difficulties are likely to lead to unmet needs. Service providers also suggested that these differences in typical coping strategies resulted in boys being more vulnerable to disciplinary exclusion. Currently, exclusion is often the trigger which allows an individual access to support.

Earlier research has focused on the peer pressures which boys, in particular, experience and which may serve as a negative influence on school achievement. Attitudes towards academic success among some boys have been found to deteriorate as they get older (Whitelaw et al., 2000). Researchers have also observed the complex and sometimes conflicting pressures which African Caribbean boys experience both from their peers and from teachers and schools (Mac an Ghaill, 1994; Sewell, 1997 and 2001). Working-class boys in particular are thought to 'behave badly' in response to academic failure and poor employment prospects (Arnot et al., 1999).

Some service providers in our study attributed greater disciplinary problems among boys to different cultural pressures and expectations on boys and girls. They saw these pressures as having an impact on both behaviour and academic achievement. They argued that whereas, for boys, gaining 'street cred' and maintaining a particular image were likely to have a negative impact on behaviour and achievement, among girls there was a greater acceptance of school authority. Two different deputy headteachers made the following observations:

I think it has a lot to do with street cred . . . more so for boys. There's the macho image thing. I've got to show that I'm big and strong . . . and the business of it being cool not to care.

Girls do better because it is more the accepted norm in school for girls to work hard and do their homework, whereas it's not cool that boys do their homework and show that they are keen and enthusiastic.

Such views are consistent with the findings of previous research, particularly that which addresses the needs and experiences of boys. As Arnot and her colleagues observe: 'Schoolwork and academic scholarship have been portrayed by some boys as feminised and in conflict with emergent masculinities' (Arnot *et al.*, 1999: 155). While both boys' and girls' behaviour and responses at school are likely to be shaped by dominant discourses about masculinity (Epstein *et al.*, 1998; Arnot *et al.*, 1999), we also note that more research needs to be undertaken if we are to fully understand girls' experiences and responses to schooling. Girls, in particular, remain in danger of being perceived as a homogeneous grouping.

The girls in our study agreed that girls, for example, are less direct in their challenges to authority because they 'don't want to get into trouble', while among some boys, 'getting into trouble' is viewed positively:

> If the boys go on report they think they're good . . . they think they've got an attitude and it's cool and girls see it as a put down.
>
> (Nicole, mainstream school)

These girls had slightly different perspectives from those of service providers. Rather than see themselves and their male peers as subject to particular pressures, they used the concept of 'reputation' as a key factor influencing their behaviour and that of boys. They sought to define what constitutes a desirable reputation for boys and for girls. A good reputation for a boy would include:

> To have slept with loads of girls, be suspended from school, not to do homework, cheek all the teachers . . . they think that's good 'cause then all their friends will be saying, 'Oh, he's good he is'.
>
> (Kim, mainstream school)

Girls on the other hand:

> Well, they've got to be, they can't let themselves be pushed

around . . . yet they've got to be friendly, and it helps if they're pretty and all that.

(Fiona, mainstream school, no exclusions)

Having 'an attitude' and being physical was seen as an important part of a boy's reputation, while for girls physical appearance was seen as important and a point of potential criticism from other girls. These differences relate to differences in the social construction of masculinity and femininity, with pressure on both boys and girls to behave in accordance with gender prescribed norms (Hey, 1997; Epstein and Johnson, 1998).

Interpersonal conflict and bullying

Some service providers attributed higher rates of exclusion and consequent access to additional supports among boys partly to gender differences in the ways that issues of bullying or interpersonal conflict are resolved. As one student expressed it:

Boys are more violent. They're always fighting.

(Kim, mainstream school)

In particular, physical acting out was seen as requiring a specific school intervention. Girls cited bullying as a direct cause of exclusion (see chapter 4), yet both girls and professionals acknowledged that the types of bullying engaged in by girls were more likely to be verbal and psychological. As such, it is less visible (and possibly regarded in many schools as less serious) and so less likely to be addressed by school authorities.

The girls also spoke of gender differences in both the typical content of disputes with peers and the way in which such disputes are resolved. Disputes between boys typically revolve around girlfriends (as property), money owed, the breaking of social norms (for example, 'grassing' on someone) or not sticking to the rules of a game, and would commonly be resolved through a physical fight. For girls, a gossip culture focusing on other girls' physical appearance or sexual activities was much more common, with name-calling, starting rumours and changing social alliances being responses to disputes.

[Boys] they fight about girls, like Nathan was with one girl and they are like fighting, 'no she's mine, no she's mine', treating us like objects.

(Kim, mainstream school)

Just like say there's rumours going round about some other girl that will have kissed your boyfriend or something like that . . . silly things like that, that might not even be true . . . just rumours that go round the school that just get people into an argument.

(Rachael, PRU, permanently excluded from mainstream school)

Whatever the issue, the girls identified gender differences in the way that conflicts were typically resolved. Boys were perceived as being more likely to resort to physical violence, while girls were viewed as more likely to resort to 'bitchiness' or verbal and psychological bullying. One of the students sought to explain the differences in boys' and girls' behaviour in terms of broader socio-cultural processes:

If they [boys] are like having an argument with someone, they have to fight them. They've got to be seen like as good in the eyes of their friends, and they think they'll get respect from everyone by fighting and stuff from their classmates. Girls, they can think about things before they do it, and they don't fight as much, they're just more bitchy towards each other.

(Fiona, mainstream school)

While these perceived gender differences in behaviours are likely to be experienced to different degrees by different pupils, the girls' reports confirm that schooling is often experienced in significantly different ways by girls and by boys. The implications of these differences in terms of the distribution of resources to support girls raise key questions about access and equity.

Accessing appropriate provision

Many service providers argued that girls and boys have the same or similar needs but that, under pressure, teachers and schools prioritise overtly disruptive behaviour, which is more characteristic of boys. As the manager of the behaviour support service in one LEA explained:

The provision that is on offer is equally accessible to girls and boys. Gender barriers are not there in the same way that they used to be, at least, not overtly. Technically, if you looked at the provision and referral criteria, you would say that we had constructed an open system that would meet everybody's needs.

In practice, a different picture emerges. This same interviewee used a running race metaphor to explain why she thinks more boys access additional supports:

> Once you get to the starting line, things are equal but certain groups seem more likely to get to the starting line. The fact that you get ten boys and one girl at the starting line is the point at which you have to start asking the questions. The hyperactive, challenging boy who can't concentrate, who is dropping things, who is thumping somebody on the back every time he walks past them, or the disorganised, ill-equipped student who is nicking everybody else's ruler or pencil – those sorts of behaviours have to be dealt with quickly and effectively because they are disrupting your lesson. If you suspect that somebody in the back row is not learning because they have been staring out the back window for the last twenty minutes, or they never get their homework done, you will find the time to sort it . . . eventually . . . but actually, they are not doing any harm, and are certainly not disrupting the lesson . . . so it's easy to overlook these sorts of behaviours.

While acknowledging that there are highly disruptive girls, and also quiet but troubled boys, participants thought that in general the second range of behaviours are more prevalent among girls, and the former, more prevalent among boys. This makes it easier to overlook some of the difficulties that girls are experiencing. One interviewee gave an example which vividly illustrates how a girl may be in difficulties and effectively self-exclude, without necessarily getting the support she may need at school:

> There is someone I am working with at the moment . . . she's very emotionally distressed, as shown by crying, worrying, refusing to do her schoolwork and those sorts of things. Whilst the school are concerned about her, it's not as pressing as a six foot kid who's throwing desks about.
>
> (educational psychologist)

This same respondent went on to argue that self-exclusion, where a student is in school but not getting full access to the curriculum, needs to be seen as a behaviour problem and a cause for concern and action:

> At one end is the quiet reserved pupil who is not making any demands on the teacher. They are not accessing the curriculum but they are also not creating any behaviour difficulties. To me that is a behaviour problem and their needs are being overlooked.

Another educational psychologist confirmed our perception that this form of exclusion was more likely to be experienced by girls:

> The withdrawn child sitting quietly at the back is more likely to be female and is in a sense excluded.

Current definitions of 'problem behaviour', together with the everyday pressures faced by schools mean that physically and verbally aggressive students tend to generate some action on the part of the school. Such action, including disciplinary exclusion, may in turn generate support for some of these students. Girls' behaviours typically tend to be overlooked and they are consequently far less likely to access support. The result is a gendered process of needs identification and gendered patterns of intervention and provision (Crozier and Anstiss, 1995; Daniels et al., 1999; Keenan et al., 1999; Lloyd and O'Regan, 2000). As some of our interviewees imply, current processes of needs identification must be broadened to encompass a wider range of behaviours.[7] The range of indicators which help teachers and other professionals to identify students in difficulty needs to be broadened to take into consideration the experiences of girls and young women as well as those of boys and young men.

Similarly the types of support available need to be extended so that girls can access appropriate provision. Service providers argued that educational alternatives tend to be male orientated and cater for male needs. For example, they highlighted work experience placements and FE college courses which focus on traditionally male interests.[8] They also cited placements and programmes where physical or outdoor activities were favoured over more academic or social ones:

I'm thinking about the Key Stage 4 alternatives. I have an impression that a lot of the things that are organised are more appealing for boys, things like painting and decorating, car mechanics, bricklaying, woodwork, carpentry. All those kinds of things, now they are traditional male things. I do know a girl who has gone to painting and decorating and has had a great time. I think it's improving, but for girls it mainly seems to be hairdressing and health and beauty and if you are not into that then you're a bit stuck.

(education welfare officer)

While programmes continue to cater more for the needs of boys it is likely that boys will continue to be advantaged over girls.

A second difficulty arises when girls are allocated places on a scheme where the vast majority of other participants are boys:

I think the biggest issue for girls in our centres is that they are largely male environments. If we didn't have our school refusers who are predominantly girls, we would have some centres where it was almost all boys.

(member of behaviour support team)

Service providers also noted the lack of Emotional and Behavioural Difficulties (EBD) places for girls, with much EBD provision catering exclusively for boys. As one educational psychologist noted:

In my job I pick up girls with Statements in relation to behaviour difficulties and I think that probably nationally the provision for those girls is poor.

She explained that a number of EBD schools are for boys only. Where they are mixed, it is often inappropriate to place one or two girls among a larger group of boys. As a consequence:

Sometimes they [girls] end up getting educated in a residential school [extra-district placement] because there is nowhere else.

(educational psychologist)

Alternatively, girls statemented for EBD tend to be returned to the mainstream because there are so few alternatives for them

(Crozier and Anstiss, 1995). Leaving debates about the appropriateness and effectiveness of specialist EBD schools to one side, girls' access to such provision is clearly extremely limited partly as a result of the gender imbalance. These two issues – alternative provision catering more for the needs of boys and more boys accessing such provision – inevitably create a self-perpetuating cycle making it even more difficult to refer girls to such support.

Both girls and professionals identified a number of ways in which girls avoid involvement with school disciplinary procedures, either intentionally or because their behaviours and responses to school do not attract the attention of professionals, working under pressure and with a gendered view of what constitutes a behavioural problem. Professionals acknowledge that girls do not have fewer needs than boys in schools but rather that their needs tended to go unrecognised and unmet. At the same time, the loud and physical nature of many boys' behaviour cannot easily be ignored or overlooked. Consequently, more boys are subject to disciplinary sanctions, which in turn enable them to get greater access to support than their female classmates. As data in subsequent chapters will confirm, this inequitable use of resources, particularly in the light of the government's aim of reducing social exclusion, is highly questionable. Achieving positive change will require targeting not just how we teach in schools but also considering what sort of support we provide and how we think about what it is to be male and female.

Chapter 4

Success and survival

In this chapter we examine how girls manage their schooling, exploring the concepts of survival and success. We report on girls' aspirations and their expectations of school. We examine the pressure to succeed as well as the barriers, processes and procedures that need to be negotiated by students in order to survive the everyday experience of school. We consider how girls react when things go wrong, for example when they encounter problems of bullying, racism or difficulties in learning or in relationships. We report on the strategies which girls adopt and the people they turn to for help. Strategies such as withdrawal from learning and truancy are discussed, together with their consequences.

Defining success

Interestingly, and in line with other research into students' expectations of school (Lloyd and O'Regan, 1999; Osborn, 1999; Benjamin, 2000; Pomeroy, 2000), the girls in our study defined success in school primarily, but not exclusively, in terms of achieving good examination grades. In this respect their views were in line with official discourse which defines school effectiveness largely in terms of academic indicators. The girls viewed schooling as important and individual academic success as desirable:

> Education is important. If you don't come to school then you've got nothing. You can't just go to college, you need to have GCSEs and everything at school.
>
> (Anna, self-excluding and permanently excluded student, attending PRU)

Almost all of the girls acknowledged a link between good GCSE grades, post-school training opportunities and better employment prospects. Even those who had experienced significant difficulties wanted 'an education' and some went so far as to express regret at missing periods of schooling through truancy. Students who were being educated in a pupil referral unit (PRU) thought it important that they could still do some GCSEs and valued what they perceived as a second chance. Several were convinced that had they stayed in a mainstream school they would have achieved nothing. One who had missed considerable amounts of schooling explained why she no longer truanted:

> 'Cause it ain't right. If you're going to have a day off school you're going to miss out. I just used to wag it all the time but it wasn't a good thing. It's just that the more you wag it, then the less education you're getting . . . the less chance of you doing your GCSEs and A levels and getting a job.
>
> (Anna, permanently excluded student)

For the majority of these girls academic success was seen in terms of its extrinsic rewards, namely, improved life choices and the opportunity to secure better paid employment:

S1: If you do well in your exams that's good 'cause you can get a good job. I just think it leads to a good job.
S2: It's about options and choices really. It's like if you go to college and university and all that then you'll get the job you want . . . and you'll probably get higher pay.

> (group interview, mainstream school)

When one girl suggested that it was possible to find work without qualifications a fellow student quickly pointed out that such work would be low paid:

S1: It's important not to get kicked out so you can get a job.
S2: But you can still get a job anyway.
S1: Yeah . . . like a little £50 a week job.

> (group interview, PRU)

Although these girls made an explicit link between higher qualifications and better pay, the emphasis placed on 'options and choices' suggests a parallel concern with job satisfaction and fulfilment. They anticipated their future employment both in terms of extrinsic rewards (good pay) and intrinsic benefits (enjoyment and fulfilment).

There was a tendency among our interviewees to take schoolwork more seriously as they approached their GCSE years, when they often experienced increased pressure from parents and teachers to perform academically. Some girls struggled to reconcile the demands of homework with other pressures on their time, including part-time employment and their desire to spend time socialising with friends. The challenge of balancing these conflicting demands was a theme running through a number of interviews:

S1: It's just like you spend most of your life at school right, you do all work during the day and then they expect you to take loads home and it's not like 20 minutes, it's like a couple of hours.
S2: And every teacher thinks their subject is the most important.
S3: Personally, I wish I could just take two weeks off school and just work every day at home getting just my assignments done, because I swear that's how long it would take me.

> (group interview, mainstream school)

One girl, who needed particular examination grades for entry into her preferred sixth-form course, echoed the views of a number of others in terms of meeting family expectations and not 'letting them down':

> I have been quite successful but recently the nearer I've got to my mocks and my GCSEs, my grades have gone down. I need at least 5 Cs. And there's pressure from the family [to] get high grades and if I don't get them I'm worried that I'm letting them down and that.
>
> (Julie, mainstream school, several internal exclusions)

Julie was exceptional in attending a school where the intake reflected a wider social mix. Most of the girls we interviewed were from schools where the intake was largely or exclusively working-class. This pressure to perform was a dominant theme but the extent to which it was felt varied both from school to school and between individuals within the same educational setting.

While the desire for high grades was evident across our sample of interviewees, a minority of students conveyed a sense of having lost hope of realising this goal. Among such students were those in low sets who believed that achieving good grades was beyond their reach.[1] For those students who are unable to attain the expected academic standards, whether as a result of learning difficulties or circumstantial factors that had had a negative impact on their attainment, the widely accepted narrow definition of success at school is problematic.[2] Difficulties in managing the curriculum and the associated feelings of failure were often exacerbated by the coping strategies such students employed, namely, self-exclusion or withdrawal from learning.

Two students reflected on the degree of personal responsibility which they felt students need to take if they are to achieve academic success. The first, who had dropped out of school as result of bullying, presented her changed views of truancy and its consequences:

> I think it's up to them, but at the end of it, it's them who are missing out. It's them who are not getting their education to get a good job and that, 'cause these days you do need a qualification.
>
> (Belinda, self-excluder, now educated in PRU)

The second, who had felt totally isolated as a result of severe physical and psychological bullying, referred to her growing determination to succeed which enabled her to overcome her own behavioural difficulties:

> After I got in trouble the first time it didn't feel like I mattered so then I kept on doing it but then I just thought that at the end of the day I want to get out of here and do my GCSE and pass it and do what I want to do in life, so I'm now just trying my best.
>
> (Daniela, mainstream school, several fixed-term exclusions)

In fact, Daniela's problems were finally addressed when her mother sought police intervention after an assault, following a period of bullying which the family felt the school had failed to tackle. Daniela explained her changed attitude partly in terms of her greater maturity and partly in terms of the more caring approach now shown by some teachers. Her mother suggested that improved teacher expectations now matched the high academic expectations she had of her own daughter. Daniela was now working hard for her GCSEs and hoped to go on to A levels and to university. The new consistent approach between home and school had had a positive and motivating effect.

Students accepted some responsibility for their own learning and achievement, but also placed considerable responsibility on their teachers. One group of girls expressed their frustration at a change of teacher halfway through the year and at the new teacher's inability to control the class. The students feared this was likely to have a direct impact on their examination performance. The underlying feeling in the group was of pressure to perform:

S1:   I have him for science and I'm sorry but I think that's really bad the way that the school have swopped science teachers and I mean, come on, we're supposed to be preparing for our GCSE and I cannot concentrate in that class and I really pray to God that I do not fail.

S2:   I mean you know when you're doing experiments, like with liver or something like that, you'd have liver being thrown around the room and you felt really unsafe and you know, you can't concentrate on . . . there's no way you'll pass a GCSE in a class like that.

(group interview, mainstream school)

With the exception of two students, all the girls in mainstream schools were doing a full range of GCSE courses. Those in alternative provision such as a PRU or college placement were enrolled in a more limited number of GCSE courses. The girls' expectations of examination success were very mixed. Some clearly expected to do well, others were hopeful but less certain, and a smaller group expected few, if any, A–C grades. All those in alternative provision appeared highly motivated and acknowledged adult assistance and support in accessing information about future education and training opportunities. Their experiences contrasted sharply with the minority of girls in mainstream schools who had little hope of gaining GCSEs and who had few ideas and little information about post-school opportunities.

Alongside academic performance, some girls placed emphasis on the social aspects of school. They considered friendship and the development of social skills an important outcome of school attendance:

You learn a lot of lessons from school about life and friends. You learn relationships with people . . . you learn how to handle different types of people.

(Cheryl, mainstream school, numerous internal exclusions)

Nicole and Kim agreed about the importance of friendship, placing it alongside 'doing your best', something which students and parents judged to be important:

S1:   For the exams to come through.
S2:   For me to have done as well as I thought I would.
S1:   And to be able to get a job because I've got good qualifications.
S2:   And friendships.
S1:   You meet most of your friends at school. They follow you through life don't they, and help you.
S2:   No matter what anyone says, if you've got your friends there then you're always all right.

(Nicole and Kim, mainstream school, no exclusions, some truancy)

Girls' career aspirations covered a wide field including professions such as medicine and law, but most girls were aiming for non-professional occupations and only a minority expected to go to university. This may reflect the working-class communities to which most interviewees belonged. Other researchers have identified a range of factors influencing the educational outcomes, aspirations and employment opportunities of those from working-class backgrounds. The various ways in which gender, ethnicity, and class intersect are somewhat complex. For example, it has been claimed that the attitudes of some working-class mothers have had a negative impact on their daughters' aspirations and achievements (Plummer, 2000). Yet other research has suggested that working-class mothers often positively influence their daughter's attitudes towards academic success (Mann, 1998). Recent research suggests that certain British Muslim families may place considerable emphasis on girls' higher education, regardless of class (Ahmad, 2001). Ahmad's findings support our earlier research which suggests that British Muslim women often have high educational aspirations for their daughters, regardless of their own educational achievements or class background (Osler and Hussain, 1995). For South Asian families more generally the concept of *izzat* (honour, reputation) continues to influence and regulate behaviour and norms, particularly, but not exclusively, those of girls and women (Wilson, 1978; Osler, 1989). Both boys and girls may acquire *izzat* through educational and career success. The academic success of girls within one family may provoke a sense of competition and similar aspirations for the daughters of other families within the same networks.

Among the girls we interviewed for this study, those from minority ethnic communities tended to have somewhat higher aspirations than their white peers, despite coming from broadly similar working-class backgrounds. Most were aiming for higher education and for professional careers. It would appear that minority ethnic parents more generally recognise the need for their daughters to be well qualified with good career opportunities. They recognise a need, first, to establish an advantage in the labour market in order to overcome the disadvantages of racial discrimination and, second, to have some protection against potential marriage breakdown (Osler, 1997c and 1999a).

A further trend was the gendered nature of the girls' aspirations, with child-care, beautician, hairdressing, clerical and retail work, fashion design, flight attendant and nurse being common goals. Girls' choice of traditionally feminine occupations has been well documented (Paechter, 1998; Arnot *et al.*, 1999; Macrae and Maguire, 2000) along with the consequences of women being over-represented in lower paid occupations (Collins *et al.*, 2000a). Young women who leave school with few educational qualifications or none are at greater risk of longer-term unemployment and social exclusion than their male peers (Collins *et al.*, 2000a). Our research supports Jackson's (1998) findings that:

> Many girls still lack confidence, often have low self-esteem and have limited educational and work aspirations. A positive action programme in schools still needs to work creatively on raising girls' low expectations.
>
> (Jackson, 1998: 91)

In fact, government agencies have acknowledged that (some) girls' apparent academic success hides a more complex problem of apparent underachievement in post-16 opportunities:

> While girls are now achieving better academic results than boys at age 16, there is little evidence to indicate that this is leading to

improved post-school opportunities in the form of training, employment, career development and economic independence for the majority of young women.

(OFSTED/ EOC, 1996: 22)

Despite this realisation and the government's rhetoric linking educational and training opportunities to social inclusion, very little attention has in fact been given to the particular needs of girls.

School organisation, relationships and security

We now explore those factors which the girls considered to be critical to their success at school. Some are institutional and to do with the way in which schools are organised and managed. Others are individual and relate to a student's personal skills, resources and abilities. Difficulties arise when there is a mismatch between the demands of a particular situation, whether this be academic or relational, and the personal or other resources available to respond to those demands.

Structural and organisational factors such as coping with large classes, the use of sets and the formality of the teacher–student relationship were problematic for some students. Girls suggested that large classes invariably meant less personal contact and greater friction between teacher and students:

> I think that in the mainstream school, if the classes were smaller, the teacher would be able to cope with the classes . . . and if they respected the pupils, they would get respect back.
>
> (group interview, PRU)

In one school, where classes were over one hour in duration and the timetable was structured with double periods, girls complained of teacher difficulties in class management. Concerns were also expressed about disciplinary procedures, particularly when these were perceived as being applied inconsistently, and about rules relating to school uniform, 'out-of-bound' areas and lack of access to a warm indoor place on cold days. Many girls looked forward to college, where they anticipated that relationships with tutors would be based on mutual respect:

When you leave school and go to college, they treat you personally.
> (group interview, mainstream school)

A number of students had encountered problems in relationships with teachers, although this was usually with some rather than all teachers. Such difficulties, even with a single teacher, can have a considerable impact on a student's learning and well-being. When the problem was extreme this invariably led to the student missing classes or whole days of school, whether as a result of formal disciplinary procedures or self-exclusion. Issues of respect, trust, teacher competence, unfair or inconsistent treatment and high teacher turnover played a part in hindering the formation of positive relationships with teachers.

Difficulties in managing the demands of the curriculum contributed to relationship difficulties, as did pressure to perform and work-related anxieties:

When I asked her [the teacher] for help she wouldn't help me. When I didn't do my work because I couldn't get any help she shouted at me.
> (Joanne, fixed-term and internal exclusions)

These difficulties are often accentuated in the case of students with special educational needs, particularly when these needs remain undiagnosed and unmet:

Some people . . . if they have problems with like dyslexia and stuff, they are too shy to admit it because of what their friends will say, so they go on pretending that they can do the things and they're not getting the right help because no one knows they've got problems.
> (group interview, mainstream school)

Justice

Perceived or actual injustice was a common concern among our interviewees. Examples were given of students who were punished for something they did not do and of disciplinary processes which were enacted without due consideration being given to contributory factors. One student reported how she was given a fixed-term exclusion for becoming involved in a fight, after being subjected to bullying. Yet the bullying was neither acknowledged nor addressed. Another student recalled how she acquired a bad reputation after transferring to a school her sister had previously attended. She acknowledged some inappropriate behaviour but felt things might have been different had she attended a different school:

> My mum thinks that I got picked on by the teachers 'cause my sister went to the same school and she was like naughty and that, so as soon as I got there they thought I was the same as my sister. They didn't give me a chance. It was like everything that happened was my fault . . . so it made me want to be naughty.
> (Rachael, fixed-term and permanent exclusions, PRU)

Most interviewees were unaware that for both boys and girls, black students are more vulnerable to disciplinary exclusion than their white peers (Osler and Hill, 1999). A minority of interviewees, from both minority and white communities, perceived that there was a racial dimension to this, citing examples of teachers they believed treated black students more harshly. One white student explained:

> Say there's a big group of us, like five black kids and six white kids, you can guarantee they'll pick out the black before they come to the white. They always think the black kids are bad . . . have done something before the white kids have.
> (Katrina, mainstream school, fixed-term exclusions)

Some girls suggested that reputation and physical appearance influenced how both teachers and fellow students viewed particular black students and affected how their behaviour was interpreted. A mixed-heritage student suggested that the greater visibility of black students (in particular being 'big and black') meant that they are perceived as threatening:

> They [black pupils] are easy targets . . . cause they're always wearing hats around school and wear big jackets and things.
> (Tina, mainstream school, fixed-term exclusions)

One black girl explained how she had to live with the reputation of being someone 'not to mess with':

The reputation I've got isn't true any more. Like some people see me as a bully, but they don't know me. They think, 'cause I hang round with this other girl, and she's like half-caste and she's tall, quite tall like me . . . I think just 'cause we're tall and we're black that we're scary. That's how I feel that I'm viewed by some people in school. They'll think we're bullies but I know I'm not anyway.

> (Daniela, mainstream school, fixed-term exclusions)

She later emphasised how there are, in fact, considerable variations in behaviour between black students, yet she had been subject to particularly harsh discipline. A bad reputation was difficult to shrug off:

Some black kids can be more badly behaved than other black students . . . 'cause I was. I was really rude. I'm totally changed now though.

> (Daniela)

Daniela's white friend believed Daniela was still subject to particularly harsh treatment, but Daniela herself took a more positive view of her form teacher's differential treatment:

Beth: 'Cause I've come in late millions of times but they didn't say anything to me. Well he [form tutor] asks where I've been and everything, but if Daniela comes in late, she gets into trouble straight away.

Daniela: A detention or something or going down on the register or whatever . . . 'you can come and see me at break time'. But I don't think it's because my form tutor is racist or nothing. I think it's 'cause he knows how hard I'm trying and he wants me to do well . . . that's what I think it is.

Social relationships and peer exclusion

Friendships were not only seen as a source of support, but were also acknowledged as a source of tension and conflict by a number of girls. This confirms earlier research that found that young women are more likely than their male counterparts to cite interactions with peers as a source of distress in school (Pomeroy, 2000). One girl suggested that boys were easier to get on with:

> I prefer getting on with boys because I think boys are well less bitchy than girls. Girls, all they do is natter, natter, slag this person or slag that person off. Boys just take things as they go really. They'll just talk about football and that and they're really laid back.
>
> (Julie, mainstream school, internal exclusions)

The same student went on to explain the detrimental effect which social tensions between girls can have on learning:

> There's distractions from a lot of my friends. If you have a fallout with someone you don't focus on the work, you're more likely to focus on your mate and trying to make up or have a go at them or something. That would be my main problem really.
>
> (Julie)

Interviewees perceived girls as generally more critical of each other than boys are, particularly in relation to physical appearance or real or perceived sexual activity. They argued girls are 'catty' and 'bitchy' with one another, tending to have long drawn out verbal/emotional fights, whereas boys were likely to resolve their differences more quickly through a physical fight:

> Boys are always fighting . . . but it depends though . . . sometimes you just see them like they have a little row and like they're friends again the next day, but with girls it lasts longer. They don't speak for ages like.
>
> (Rachael, permanently excluded, PRU)

Reported disagreements among girls centred on starting false rumours, name-calling or 'slagging each other off' and taking each others' boyfriends. Some points of conflict may have occurred some time in the past but are not forgotten:

> Yeah, she'll bring up past things that I sometimes regret doing and it's normally about boys. I'll end up screaming at her and she'll scream back at me, we'll have an argument.
>
> (Julie, mainstream school)

Loyalty between close friends might be thrown into question if one of them appeared to neglect the friendship in favour of a relationship with a boy. Two friends sought to identify sources of conflict:

Nicole: Reputations, friendships . . . she's my friend first . . . she's not your friend . . . taking friends off each other, yeah.

Julie: And boyfriends. Like your best mate thinks: 'Well she spends loads of time with her boyfriend, she ain't got no time for me', and starts arguing and things.

Social allegiances were critical. As Julie explained, a sense of loyalty to one's group appeared to prohibit getting on with others until a particular dispute had been resolved:

Girls always support each other. Whenever you have an argu-ment or something, there's always sides to it and there's always one girl and her mates and the other girl with her posse of mates on the other side and then as soon as the main girls make up, the groups are all right again. It always happens like that.

(Julie, mainstream school)

Our study confirms earlier research that relationships are clearly a valued and important aspect of school life for girls, yet events such as fallouts with friends, social harassment or being socially excluded are traumatic for those involved and can have a detri-mental effect on concentration and learning (Hey, 1997). That girls' friendships tend to be closer and more intimate than those of boys means that the effects of name-calling or social exclusion may be more severe for girls than they are for boys (Stanley and Arora, 1998).

Bullying and exclusion

Our research revealed that girls saw bullying as a major contribu-tory factor leading to various forms of exclusion from school. They gave numerous examples of how girls had absented them-selves from school in an attempt to avoid bullying and also illus-trated how attempts to deal with bullies, such as retaliating or lashing out at the bully, can lead directly to disciplinary exclusion. Although there has been extensive research on bullying, the links between bullying and exclusion have not formed a central theme of this research. In contrast to girls, the professionals we interviewed did not make the link between girls' exclusion from school and bullying. It appeared that levels of awareness among service providers as to its damaging effects on girls' learning and educational opportunities were low.

> I've got two friends who don't come to school sometimes 'cause they like get kind of bullied and they just go home. They don't really stay home because they want to wag . . . it's because of the bullying.
>
> (Belinda, self-excluding pupil, PRU)

There is growing recognition of the detrimental effects of bullying, including the verbal and psychological bullying which the girls in this study highlighted. A third of girls and a quarter of boys are at some time afraid of going to school because of bullying (DfEE, 1999c), suggesting that the detrimental effects of bullying are felt most acutely by girls. It is unclear whether girls experience more bullying or are more sensitive to it. Given the greater importance which girls place on friendship and social networks (Hey, 1997; Stanley and Arora, 1998), the latter seems quite likely.

It is generally recognised that boys are more likely to be involved in physical bullying and girls in verbal or psychological bullying (Stanley and Arora, 1998; Schools Health Education Unit, 2000; OFSTED, 2001). Most attention has focused on males or on explicitly aggressive behaviour (Sutton, 2001), with relatively little attention paid to verbal forms of harassment, such as name-calling, despite this being among the most prevalent forms of bullying in schools (Crozier and Dimmock, 1999).

Official guidance highlights the distress that can result from bullying:

> The emotional distress caused by bullying in whatever form – be it racial, or as a result of a child's appearance, behaviour or special educational needs, or related to sexual orientation – can prejudice school achievement, lead to lateness or truancy and in extreme cases, end with suicide.
>
> (DfEE, 1999a: 4.29)

Without exception the girls in our study identified bullying as an issue for them personally or for fellow students. They reported that *any* difference is liable to be targeted, including physical attributes or mannerisms, clothing, the existence of special educational needs and one's personal reputation or reputation of parents, including rumoured or actual sexual activity. Race and country of origin were also reported as a specific focus of bullying. Halima, a student of South Asian heritage, reported her experiences:

> I don't think there should be racism in school. I was bullied when I was in Year 7 . . . um, you eat curries, you shouldn't be here, this isn't your country and things like that and I didn't really like that.
>
> (Halima, mainstream school, no exclusions)

There was some indication that asylum seekers, recent migrants and students of South Asian descent are more likely to experience racial harassment than those of African descent:

> I haven't seen lots of bullying towards black people . . . I see it towards Asian people and people from different countries.
>
> (Julie, white pupil, mainstream school)

Interviewees identified three categories of bullying: physical (hitting, spitting, throwing things, slamming door in face, damage to property); verbal (name-calling, 'slagging off'); and psychological (starting false rumours, whispering campaigns, 'blanking', giving looks). Girls perceived themselves as typically involved in verbal or psychological bullying. As one participant put it:

> If a boy's going to bully he'll use violence. Girls do it mentally because they're clever. They know it hurts more.
>
> (Beth, mainstream school, no exclusions)

Both girls and parents reported detrimental effects on sleeping and eating patterns and the ability to concentrate. They provide some indication of the level of stress produced by bullying:

> Whenever I got home and tried to tell somebody I just burst out in tears . . . and I was so tired because I got so upset over everything in the end I was just falling asleep.
>
> (Andrea, mainstream school, no exclusions)

Even when bullying and its impact on an individual is recognised, schools encounter difficulties in addressing the psychological bullying more typically engaged in by girls:

> I was bullied at this school for three years . . . and the teachers
> . . . I did go to them and my parents as well and like it helped
> a bit, but they couldn't suspend her or nothing 'cause she
> hadn't physically touched me, but to me it wasn't about what
> she was doing physically . . . she was just destroying me
> mentally.
>
> (Daniela, mainstream school, fixed-term exclusions)

Some girls gave examples of teachers intervening effectively to
stop bullying, but more often interviewees thought that teachers
could and should do more. According to the girls, bullying tended
to take place when a teacher temporarily left a class, during breaks,
or before and after school. The more 'subtle' psychological forms of
bullying practised by girls accentuate the invisibility of these processes. 'Blanking' or social exclusion from a group can be extremely
distressing to experience but very difficult for an outsider to detect.
Even audible verbal bullying such as name-calling or other teasing can
be difficult to identify because it often involves an element of humour
and to an outside observer (or even the recipient) the intentions,
hurtful or otherwise, may be ambiguous and somewhat difficult
to interpret (Crozier and Dimmock, 1999). The hidden nature of
such bullying poses a challenge for schools in addressing the issue
adequately.

Many girls expressed the view that there is little support for victims of bullying and that the impact or seriousness of bullying is
underestimated. Several girls reported parents having to intervene
on their behalf before the school took the bullying seriously and a
resolution was reached. In two cases, resolution required the
involvement of the police.

A number of girls identified a link between bullying and exclusion. For example, Daniela was excluded for getting into a fight
with another girl. She thought that the bullying that precipitated
her angry outburst and the racial harassment to which she was
subjected were overlooked by the school in their decision to exclude
her:

> This girl kept on making fun of me and saying that she was
> going to beat me up. It was in this one lesson, right from
> the start to the finish of the lesson . . . and there were racial
> comments as well, calling me 'black bitch' and stuff.
>
> (Daniela)

Other interviewees argued it was unfair that some bullies get to stay in school while their 'victims' might be excluded or choose to stay home:

> Yes, because some of the time that's why they get excluded, it's because they've been bullied . . . like they get bullied, and then they've got it all bottled up inside and just let it out at the wrong time.
>
> (Kim, mainstream school)

Kim gave the example of boys taunting some girls until one of them eventually reacted and was excluded. She concluded:

> That's wrong, because the lad's still there to do it to another girl . . . but the girl wouldn't have to retaliate if it wasn't happening in the first place.
>
> (Kim)

Strategies employed by girls to deal with bullying included keeping it to themselves, seeking support from a friend or adult or attempting to avoid the bully, for example, by self-exclusion from school or particular classes or hiding in the library during breaks. Verbal or physical retaliation and becoming a bully were other responses. Talking it through and resolving the issue directly with the perpetrator was reported on rare occasions. In these cases, perpetrator and victim were part of the same social group.

The degree to which an individual was able to overcome bullying usually depended on her personal resources, including confidence, self-esteem and social skills. Some participants suggested that the way that some girls responded in social situations contributed to their experiences of bullying:

> It got really bad before they did anything about it. They used to follow her home and stuff and throw things at her. They never actually beat her up but I know someone that got beaten up. And Mary is one of my best friends and she didn't have any self-esteem . . . no confidence . . . she was just 'I'm scared, I'm scared'. Lucy's another one . . . she tends to say the wrong thing and she offends people. Sometimes you want to say 'Just shut up Lucy'.
>
> (Dianne, mainstream school, no exclusions)

Some strategies were considered problematic, and seeking teacher assistance was rarely an initial response. This was usually due to embarrassment, fear of making it worse, the social unacceptability of 'grassing' on someone or being unsure about which teacher to turn to:

> There's sort of two reasons [why I would not go to a teacher]. I wouldn't know which teacher to go to and anyway, it does make it worse. Say I was getting called names and I went to a teacher and the teacher went to the students who were calling me names and said stop calling this person names, that person would think it's upsetting them, I'm going to do it more.
>
> (Nicole, mainstream school)

Reservations about confiding in parents were based on similar reasons:

> They [victims of bullying] deal with it themselves. You don't tell your mum 'cause she tells the teachers, the teachers tell them off and then you get battered and that's why people don't go to school.
>
> (Louise, mainstream school, some truanting)

Sometimes those who had friends in whom they could confide hesitated out of fear that their friend would take matters into their own hands and escalate the situation, thus making it much more public and eliciting an unhelpful response from school authorities. For example, one participant responded to the continual verbal harassment of a friend by getting into a physical fight with the perpetrator. This resulted in her receiving a fixed-term exclusion. While she readily accepted the inappropriateness of assault as a way of resolving the problem, she also felt a sense of injustice that the bullying that had precipitated her outburst went unacknowledged and unaddressed.

Even when an individual had friends to turn to, bullying often resulted in feelings of isolation:

> I think it's good if you have friends to go to, I mean you lot all know me and you know that I've got a lot of friends in school, but when I was bullied I felt like I was alone. I didn't even feel like I had anyone to turn to.
>
> (Fiona, group interview, mainstream school)

Without friends, the sense of isolation was extreme. It is perhaps not surprising that self-exclusion was the chosen strategy for some pupils:

> And I was getting called fat and everything and then . . . [other students] they'd mostly swear at me and . . . it was just stupid but it really got on my nerves, so I didn't want to go.
> (Emma, long-term non-attender, in FE college placement)

Verbal and physical retaliation was another response to bullying. Not only did girls see it as ineffective but it sometimes resulted in disciplinary action including, in some cases, formal exclusion:

> I was stressing out all the time, trying to keep calm, and then I'd get provoked and shout back at people and that'd get me in trouble. Teachers would try to keep it calm but I just couldn't, I'd shout back to them and that would make it worse.
> (Sam, mainstream school, some self-exclusion)

One group of students discussed how racial harassment could lead to angry outbursts:

> S1: 'Cause they [ethnic minority pupils] probably get more name-calling.
> S2: They're provoked more.
> S1: And they end up fighting and that.
> (mainstream school group interview)

Some girls viewed physical or verbal retaliation as appropriate, believing it was important to 'stand up for yourself', or at the very least, not indicate you were intimidated:

> I think right, if you're getting bullied, if you show you're scared of them then they'll carry on, but if you stand your ground you'll be all right.
> (group interview, mainstream school)

Others expressed a determination not to assume victim status and had been successful in facing up to bullies. In the example below, the student had stopped attending school because of bullying:

In the end I just thought I'm not having any more of this, you know, they're stopping me getting the education that I want and I'm just letting them get away with it, so I just came back to school and tried to face up to it. And in the end they'll realise that you're trying to be bigger than them and so they'll stop.

(Andrea, mainstream school, no exclusions)

A few students were successful in seeking support and recognised the importance of reaching out to others:

Firstly, I think most kids would talk to their friends about it, whereas some people just lock it up and don't say anything and just try and cope with it themselves. I know that's hard, which is why I have always turned to a friend and then gone to the teachers.

(Fiona, mainstream school)

A final strategy for dealing with bullying was to become a bully. One group of girls acknowledged how they had engaged in bullying behaviour and how peer pressure can play a part in this:

Sometimes, the one that's bullying the person has usually been bullied themselves . . . so they take it out on another person. They think 'The only way I can get round this is if I can be a bully myself'.

(Nicole and Kim, group interview, mainstream school)

Usually you just go with the crowd, don't you?

(another speaker in group interview)

In two schools, girls spoke of a proactive approach to dealing with bullying that involved ensuring that all new students are made aware of the school's anti-bullying policy and are encouraged to tell a teacher, parent or friend if they become a victim. Some girls valued the support provided by an education welfare officer, staff in the 'in-school' centre or a teacher who was willing to listen. One school ran an anti-bullying group which one participant reported finding useful:

I experienced bullying in my first year but it was dealt with instantly. The school has actually got an anti-bullying club as well. Half of you don't know about it because it's all under-

ground, all secretive and everything. It's run by the school
nurse and bullying is not taken here. Everyone matters in a
school like this. That's what happened as far as personally I was
concerned.

(Daljeet, group interview, mainstream school)

Of particular significance was the variation between schools in
the extent to which they acknowledged and addressed bullying and
also the lengths to which some girls will go in order to avoid bullying. Self-exclusion was a strategy used by some girls that has clear
negative consequences in terms of their educational and social
development.

Avoiding exclusion and accessing support

The girls recruited support from a range of sources including adults,
parents, siblings and friends. There were potential difficulties with
these various sources of help that usually related to issues of trust,
confidentiality or perceived ability of the individual to make a difference. In some cases, help was not readily available or girls felt that
there was no one to whom they could turn. Despite the challenges,
many girls demonstrated considerable resourcefulness in finding
someone who would provide at least a degree of support. Those
who lacked such support were the most vulnerable to exclusion of
some form. The extent of reported non-attendance among our
interviewees through self-exclusion and other avoidance strategies
raises concerns about the amount of school being missed by some
girls.

Within school there were varying degrees of formality through
which adult support was accessed. At the most formal level was a
range of visiting professionals, such as a behaviour support worker,
social worker, education welfare officer or educational psychologist.
Access to these was limited and required a school referral. Some
girls expressed resentment at being 'sent to someone', but other
examples were given where the professional successfully engaged a
young person. Various forms of exclusion were often avoided when
girls felt an equal participant in the process and had a degree of
control over any interventions that resulted.

Other forms of support, such as a school counsellor, staff in the
'in-school' centre, a school nurse or a school-based education welfare officer were usually accessed through self-referral. A student

described the varying use of her school counsellor and the ways in which she had benefited from the service:

> Yeah, there's a couple of people in my class who use it regularly and there's other people who've just gone to her, talked to her for just one or two sessions. But there is somebody in my class who used her weekly.
>   . . . 'cause she'll give you advice and I mean it's advice you don't have to take and you can figure out your own ideas from that, but it's just a bit of encouragement and a bit of support.
>
> (Andrea, mainstream school, no exclusions)

Other informal sources of support included a form tutor, the school secretary or anyone else with whom a student had already established a relationship:

> My form teacher . . . I think it must have been during breaks and lunchtimes, I'd sit with him and tell him and he'd try and help.
>
> (Sam, mainstream school)

Whom a student chose to go to in any given circumstance varied considerably depending on such factors as the nature of the problem, the kind of help required, who was available and the potential of the individual to offer something useful:

> If the problem was a teacher I'd probably deal with it in a different way than if it was another student or something.
>
> (Cheryl, internal exclusion)

Teachers were more likely to be approached in relation to school-work or classroom difficulties, whereas a school nurse would be approached for a whole range of issues, not necessarily health related. In the example below, a student differentiates between the practical support that might be needed from an adult and the moral support which friends can provide:

> If I had a drug problem I'd go to a teacher. If I found out I was pregnant or something I'd tell my friends first. My friends well, they couldn't really help me if I was pregnant but they could come with me to test, but if I had a drug problem, I've not, but I

would actually discuss it and that with a teacher or the nurse or something.

(Anna, PRU)

The single most important factor influencing choice of support was the perceived trustworthiness of the person, whether this was a staff member, parent or friend. Trust appeared to be given to those whom they believed had a genuine interest in them, as demonstrated by their taking time to listen, give advice or render practical assistance. An established 'relationship history' through which 'trust credentials' could be established was seen as important:

> She [a teacher] knows me really well. She's just there every time something happens. Like if I've got a problem or if someone's got a problem with me, she'll just sit down and talk to me and that. She's always got time.
>
> (Daniela, mainstream school)

For these reasons, the less formal sources of support were often the most valued. Several service providers and parents suggested that the heavy workloads and demands faced by many teachers hinders the development of more personal relationships between teacher and student. A student observed:

> It tends to be the ones that aren't very important teachers that help more. Say, instead of the Head of Year helping, my music teacher helps me more. You get teachers that are a lot more understanding. Some, they'll actually listen and you'll notice that any rebel child will talk to anyone that lets them tell their story.
>
> (Dianne, mainstream school)

The girls provided examples of teachers informally stepping in to prevent a crisis. An example was given of a serious altercation between a teacher and a fellow student that was resolved through the timely and sensitive intervention of another teacher. The teacher was able to intervene because she had an established relationship of trust with the student:

> She [the student] didn't go to anyone [for help] . . . someone came to her. There was another teacher from across the room

who just came in and gently said 'Helen, do you want to come with me for a minute love?' And Helen was really stressing and she was like 'Yeah, all right' and she went out and then she [the student] said 'You see, that's how you're supposed to talk to us'. And that was it . . . she went with her and when she came back it was all sorted.

(Dianne, mainstream school)

Confidentiality was highly valued, and someone who could not be trusted with confidential information was unlikely to be approached even if student support was a central aspect of that individual's role. Those professionals who were able to establish a way of being viewed by students as distinct from the teaching staff were most likely to be effective:

In this school there's a nurse who you can see, if you have any problems you can go and speak to her. Most of them like don't because they think she's just going to go and tell all the other teachers.

(Anna, PRU)

Parents, particularly mothers, were also cited as a source of support:

With me, if I'm going to a teacher, I'm going to someone who knows me quite well and it would be either the nurse or Miss M. . . . but I prefer to go to my mum.

(Daniela, mainstream school, fixed-term exclusions)

Daniela's close relationship with her mother had been strengthened by her mother's consistent and determined support. It may well have influenced Daniela's growing determination to change her behaviour and do well at school. Her mother provided an excellent problem-solving role model, stepping in when she thought that school support had fallen short:

If the teachers can't support them, what are they supposed to do? It's left up to the parents to do something.

(Daniela's mother)

This mother's concerns about bullying were not taken seriously by the school, until she eventually went to the police and registered a complaint relating to an assault on her daughter. It was only at this point, when the police took the matter up, that the school began to provide effective support. In a second case, occurring at another school, the school authorities equally could and should have been able to address the problem. Unfortunately, in this case, the mother was not in a position to offer effective support:

> Some parents don't try with the children because they don't know how to. That was like my mum when I was bullied. My mum she tried at first and then it was breaking her down inside, she didn't even know what to do. So I was on my own and you know, that's why things have escalated and they've got worse.
>
> (Kirsty, mainstream school, no exclusions)

One risk associated with turning to a parent was the possibility of having the problem taken out of one's hands. Parental concern for a child may not always be expressed in the way a student would wish. For many girls, friends were often the first source of support. Adult assistance might only be sought after advice from a friend:

> I don't know which teacher I'd pick. I dunno. Probably, tell my mum but I wouldn't go around crying about it. She'd probably go: 'We'll have to go down the school.' Yeah. I'd probably rather talk to my friends about it than anyone else. I think I'd probably talk to my friends first.
>
> (Dianne, mainstream school)

One participant reported using Childline when in Year 7 and finding that useful. She liked the fact that it was anonymous and confidential, including that such calls do not appear on the phone-bill. She argued that this service was particularly important for those who had few friends and did not feel able to approach a trusted adult.

School avoidance and self-exclusion

Self-exclusion was a strategy engaged in by girls to manage difficulties such as antagonistic relationships with certain teachers, bullying by peers or difficulties in managing the curriculum. Both parents and girls recognised that non-attendance was a coping strategy for many such students:

> Well, I think it's because probably they don't enjoy lessons because there might be some other kids that upset them or they don't really like the teacher or don't like the lesson or get on in lessons . . . they can't do it . . . and then they think 'I can't be bothered doing this, I want to go home.'
>
> (Halima, mainstream school, no exclusions)

> She used to hate to go to school those days . . . and she was missing a lot of days. She didn't do a full week for months and that's how the welfare officer got involved.
>
> (Parent of self-excluding pupil)

Girls also truanted in response to peer relationship difficulties or to actual or anticipated disciplinary procedures:

> Well, people don't come to school if they've fell out with their friends and they're worried about what they're going to say . . . or if you've been in trouble . . . or didn't go to detention . . . they don't go to school the next day. Sometimes you don't want to go because you know you're going to be in trouble.
>
> (Anna, PRU)

While all but one of the girls reported truanting for brief periods, a smaller but significant number reported missing extended periods of school. Eight girls had ceased attending their mainstream schools altogether. In the case of one long-term truant it was both feelings of not fitting in and difficulties with the work that led to her truancy. She subsequently became the victim of bullying:

> I didn't really fit in, so I didn't want to go to school. Teachers wouldn't really help me with my work. It really started from there.
>
> (Belinda, self-excluder now being educated in PRU)

For others, truancy appeared to occur simply because the alternatives that day seemed more appealing, there was pressure from friends or detection was unlikely. Students suggested that peer culture and drug use were two factors which might contribute to truancy:

Most of the time I just went off with my mates and that, and to my friend's house 'cause he didn't go to school or anything. Most of my mates didn't go to school at that time. I didn't know many people that went to school.

(Kirsty, mainstream school)

'Cause some [students] they have more fun sitting round someone's house . . . mainly drugs as well, 'cause once you get into drugs and that, you just think 'Oh school's rubbish, you might just as well go and have fun'.

(Caroline, self-excluder with both fixed-term and permanent exclusions, mainstream school)

It is interesting that Caroline made a point of attending Art classes, even when she missed all other classes that day. She particularly disliked German, a subject in which she experienced little success. Following a move to a different part of the country she had improved her attendance and appeared to have made a successful re-integration back to formal education after missing nearly half a year of schooling. Both a different social circle and a different school appeared to have aided her re-integration.

Our findings confirm Reid's (1999) conclusions that official truancy statistics underestimate actual levels of truancy, particularly for girls. Reported strategies that resulted in unrecorded absences included post-registration truancy, getting friends to lie about their whereabouts, being physically present at school but skipping particular lessons and either forging notes or phoning in and posing as a parent reporting sickness:

When you have a day off you're meant to take a letter in with you but like most of the girls used to just write it themselves and take it in.

(Rachael, permanently excluded pupil, PRU)

Sometimes, I would go in and get my mark so I'd get a full attendance but after I got my mark I'd go home and I'd come back at lunchtime and get my mark and go back home.

(Nadine, permanently excluded pupil, PRU)

Another student suggested this was a widespread practice at her school and that despite the school having a policy of vigorously following up all absences, procedures were not applied consistently:

Well, they sent a letter home to every pupil in the school saying like if your child is bunking or they're ill or whatever, if they don't come in, we're going to phone up the parents on that morning, the first morning, to see where they are, but they never did. 'Cause my friends, they bunked and the school never phoned their mum and dad. . . . Yeah, a lot of kids will say come in for registration, bunk all lessons, come back to registration and then bunk again. Just to make the teacher think oh I'm in, 'cause they're in the register.

(Kirsty, mainstream school, no exclusions)

One student thought that at her school, boys who truanted were more closely monitored and likely to be followed up:

They send a form and stuff and you have to fill it in and say where you were and the reasons why you were not at school and stuff. I've never had to do it. Certain people, mainly the boys . . . when they wag school if they don't come back straight away then they'll get this letter.

(Andrea, mainstream school)

Levels of truancy appeared to be influenced by the school's policy and practices. At one school, measures such as CCTV cameras, random class register checks and out-of-school truancy sweeps were perceived to make detection more likely and thus reduce the frequency of certain types of truancy. At some schools, efforts to combat truancy were seen as largely ineffective.

Persistent long-term school refusers who were being educated in a PRU or college reported very high attendance in their new setting. These pupils attributed their improved attendance to a range of factors, including smaller classes, personalised relationships with staff, more support with schoolwork and a belief that staff care and have a genuine interest in them. This finding supports the view expressed by some participants that many girls who truant actually want to be at school but truant as a way of avoiding the difficulties:

There was rumours going around about her. I don't know if they were true or not . . . that she'd been sleeping around with people, stuff like that. She probably does want to be at school but she can't come because everyone's just going to take it out on her. The others just don't want to 'cause of the way they feel that day, that's all.

(Fiona, Year 10, mainstream school, no exclusions)

This student and many others drew a distinction between casual truanting by those who were bored or influenced by their friends, and more persistent non-attenders who were experiencing serious problems, such as the girl who was the subject of significant harassment because of her perceived sexual activity. They thought that pupils in the former category were more likely to truant for a lesson or sometimes a whole day because they are 'sick of school'. For the latter group, they might want to be at school but find it too difficult because it is a physically or emotionally unsafe environment.

Faking or exaggerating illness was another strategy used to avoid school or particular lessons. Sometimes the school nurse was an unknowing collaborator in this:

[They] go matron. They say they don't feel well and then they get sent to matron. I've done it before. Yeah. She'll just believe you and I've just sat there for like the whole class. The first few times it's easy, but after a while she's like: 'No – you're always coming here'.

(Louise, mainstream school, fixed-term exclusion)

Service providers also thought that more girls than boys use ill health as a way of opting out and that it is seen by students as a more legitimate way for a girl to opt out. An education officer in one LEA expressed particular concern about one school where there were very few girls formally excluded or truanting but where an unusually high number had been diagnosed with ME and were subsequently receiving part-time education in a PRU. She believed some of these girls to be school phobic and thought that closer communication between education and health services would have resulted in a more appropriate response to this phenomenon and one that was more likely to address the school and family factors that contributed to attendance difficulties.

Menstrual discomfort and emotional outbursts were described by several participants as other ways of getting out of class:

You can scream so much that they think, 'Crazy woman, let her out' sort of thing and you just get out of school and get out of lessons.

(Dianne, mainstream school, no exclusions)

School avoidance was rarely the first strategy adopted by the girls. Rather, a pattern of non-attendance would develop over time as other attempts to manage difficulties proved unsuccessful. Some interviewees who truanted for prolonged periods made a point of attending particular lessons, perhaps in a particular subject they enjoyed or with a teacher with whom they got on.

Inevitably, non-attendance often exacerbated the underlying difficulty, increasing the likelihood of further truancy. Once such a pattern was established it was sometimes difficult to change:

And then it's hard to come back . . . you're behind with work . . . can't catch up and it's easier to stay away.

(Belinda, self-excluding pupil, PRU)

Sometimes parents felt unable or unwilling to insist on attendance. Of the ten mothers who were interviewed, all of their daughters had refused to attend school for periods of time because of bullying or a conflict with a particular teacher. In each case the mother felt more could have been done in school to sort the problem out. One student illustrated how she would rather engage in conflict with her mother than face the difficulties of school:

I would see my mum [later] at my nan's but she always went mad at me, but there was nothing she could do. She knew there was no way she was getting me to go to school.

(Belinda, former self-excluder, at PRU)

It can be seen how girls employed a range of strategies to survive at school and it was only when these failed that they resorted to self-exclusion. Most welcomed the opportunity to talk to a trusted adult when difficulties arose, and those who had access to a school nurse or school counsellor tended to see the benefits of these professionals, particularly if they were not seen as too closely tied to the world of teachers. The girls we interviewed were, on the whole, determined to succeed at school and saw success largely in terms of achieving good academic results which might lead to more rewarding and better paid employment. For the small minority who saw little chance of academic success, school appeared to offer very little. Those whose self-exclusion led to alternative education in a PRU or other placement usually flourished. The support offered in the new environment often included longer-term guidance on future training and careers which girls in the mainstream rarely seemed to successfully access.

Chapter 5

Experiences of exclusion and inclusion

In this chapter we report on girls' views of exclusion as a disciplinary sanction and on their views of what makes an inclusive school. We examine alternative educational provision and consider whether it is experienced as inclusion or exclusion. Students reflect on their experiences of learning and seek to identify the characteristics of a good teacher. Their experiences and observations provide valuable insights into those factors that enable schools to be experienced as inclusive. School organisational and structural factors, pastoral support strategies, the curriculum and pedagogy all feature in their discussions. They emphasise the importance of positive relationships between teachers and students, between students themselves and also between the school and parents. Drawing on their experiences, the girls make suggestions on how schools might become more inclusive and democratic. As we have argued in chapter 2, questions of school inclusion and exclusion are questions of human rights, and one of the key features of a democratic society must be an inclusive school system. Any form of educational exclusion is inconsistent with the principles of a democratic society (Ballard, 1999).

Why exclude?

Around a quarter of the girls we interviewed had been subject to fixed-term or permanent exclusion as a disciplinary sanction, with a few more reporting internal exclusions. A smaller number (around one-fifth) had self-excluded. The students themselves tended to associate formal disciplinary exclusion, either fixed-term or permanent, with verbally abusive behaviour, regular non-compliance with school rules or teacher instructions, persistent disruption or violence. Unlawful activities such as stealing or carrying drugs were also cited by the girls as behaviours that would result in formal exclusion:

> Beating someone up, it's normally violent things. Or they're really giving it to the teacher, like swearing at them really bad and things like that. They're the sort of things you get excluded for.
>
> (Julie, mainstream school, no exclusions)

> 'Cause you're too disruptive and you just ruin it for everyone else . . . wasting the teacher's time and things like that. Also, if you bring drugs into the school . . . if you get caught with drugs or a weapon like a knife or something, then the police will be phoned and you'll be chucked out.
>
> (Anna, PRU, permanently excluded)

A prevalent theme in the girls' discussions of formal exclusion was that of perceived inconsistency in the way this sanction is applied. They argued that whether a particular incident resulted in exclusion depended not just on the seriousness of the 'offence' but also on factors such as the attitude of the particular teacher involved, the teacher's mood, the student's reputation and teacher perceptions of the student:

> S1: It depends on who you are really.
> S2: Like if you're not usually in trouble for a lot of things then they don't [exclude] but if you've been in trouble a lot before they might.
> S3: And if the teacher doesn't like you.
>
> (group interview, mainstream school)

Service providers echoed these views, with some expressing concern that there should be such inconsistencies, even within a school, in how the sanction was applied:

> You'll get someone who is excluded for something that seems incredibly minor and you wonder why on earth that exclusion has taken place or why that person was excluded and the others weren't.
>
> (youth worker)

These professionals acknowledged the difficulties in working with students who present challenging behaviour, but like the young people we interviewed, they believed that the practice of exclusion often reflected teacher stress and a lack of alternative strategies. The head of a pupil referral unit (PRU) observed inconsistencies in the way exclusion had been applied to the young people who had been referred to her. She argued that much more could be done to support students in the mainstream:

> And I've got a theory about exclusion . . . if you look at the case papers of any of our kids, what is it about the day they were excluded that was different from all the other days when they were behaving badly but were kept in school? It's always about the staff . . . about how the teachers were that day. It isn't actu-ally about how the kids were. The incident that got them excluded isn't all that different from all the other incidents that happened to them before. I think it's about tolerance and lack of alternatives to exclusion.
>
> (head of PRU)

The girls were also aware of varying exclusion rates between schools, attributing this more to how schools managed and sup-ported students than to the students themselves. A number of par-ticipants readily acknowledged instances where their own behaviour had been inappropriate, but they also argued that some schools needed a broader range of strategies for dealing with students who were liable, for example, to lose their temper. In other words, they tended to place responsibility on the school for failing to resolve problems and were unwilling to locate the problem exclusively within the individual:

> Some schools have better ways of dealing with things when there are problems, like bringing parents in.
>
> (group interview, mainstream school)

Opinions varied as to why some schools exclude more students than others, with many students suggesting that schools have differ-ent standards of 'strictness'. Some interviewees thought that it looked good for a school to exclude students as this implies strict-ness and an expectation of high standards of behaviour, while others thought that it looked good for a school to exclude very few pupils as this conveys competence in the management of students. Teachers who took part in one of our earlier studies of exclusion also held these contrasting views of how exclusion is perceived by parents and the general public (Osler, 1997a). Only a minority of students attributed a greater number of exclusions to the school having a greater number of 'problem' pupils. Schools which did not readily exclude were generally viewed by the girls as more accepting, tolerant and supportive of students. In the dialogue below girls were responding to a question about why they thought some schools exclude more students than others:

S1: Because the bad girls will give the school a bad name . . . and if you get rid of those ones, you can get some more people in that might be good.

S2: Yeah, but the school looks better if they don't expel people 'cause that means they can keep them in and are teaching them properly.

S3: The school I was at, they didn't like losing the pupils unless they really had to. I remember there was this one kid from Year 7, he did really play up and I still speak to my mates who go there and they still say he's there now.

(group interview, PRU)

Interestingly, this last speaker had self-excluded from that school, suggesting that the school's support structures had been less effective in addressing her particular difficulties.

One student saw her own school's low exclusion rate as a particularly positive feature and thought that this, along with the support systems in place, contributed to the generally good academic results and student behaviour:

I think [our school] is quite a fair school really and they'll give people a few chances and if they blow their chances then they'll get excluded. Some people know they've done something wrong and they'll sort that problem out so therefore there's no point in excluding them. [Other schools] they don't really give them a fair chance, they just think 'Right, you can go'.

(Julie, mainstream school, no exclusions)

Another student at the same school commented on why she thought the school used both fixed-term and permanent exclusion sparingly.

She indicated that fixed-term exclusion is of limited value as a behaviour management strategy:

> I don't know. I guess they might have come to terms with the fact that kicking them out won't help. They're just the same, or worse, when they get back. There is no point except that it will destroy their education.
>
> (Dianne, no exclusions)

In line with this, students in a different part of the country were very critical of a neighbouring school which had a high exclusion rate. It is possible that there was some resentment about their school receiving students excluded from their neighbouring school. However, they indicate that they value the efforts made by their school to support students in difficulties:

S1:   [Neighbouring school] . . . they kick them out and then we get them.
S2:   Yeah, we have all them . . . and [neighbouring school] have all the clever ones that just don't make any trouble.
S3:   They probably want a good reputation.
S2:   This school tries to help. Like if people are bad, they take them out and sit and talk to them instead of kicking them out straight away. Like they try and make them do better.

> (group interview, mainstream school)

Shortly after this interview took place, the neighbouring school received public recognition for its high academic achievements. Not surprisingly, the public image of success overlooked the school's levels of exclusion, both formal and informal. Media coverage stressed that there was no selective admissions system, yet evidence from our student interviewees and local service providers suggests secondary processes of selection were operating through the mechanism of exclusion. The students' observations, that the neighbouring school's good reputation was maintained at the expense of the students that it 'kicked out' and at the expense of their school, had a ring of truth. The neighbouring school may well have introduced some innovative initiatives to support the achievement of (some of) its students, but service providers in the area confirmed that high levels of formal and informal exclusion were also practised. The example highlights the tension created for schools in a context of competition, when 'effectiveness' is measured in very narrow terms (Ainscow *et al.*, 1999; Munn *et al.*, 2000; Florian and Rouse, 2001; Loxley and Thomas, 2001). As other researchers have noted:

> Government initiatives in education are not always compatible with moves towards inclusive education. In particular . . . a culture which seems to measure quality in terms of narrowly focused examination and test results may not acknowledge the excellent work going on in schools to support pupils experiencing difficulties.
>
> (Ainscow *et al.*, 1999: 139)

Generally speaking, the girls viewed exclusion, whether it was permanent, fixed-term or internal, as an ineffective behaviour management strategy, although some also believed it to be necessary in some cases. This was usually when disruptive behaviour impinged on the rights of others to education or when the safety of other students or teachers was threatened. Some girls suggested that the effectiveness of the sanction also depended on the parental attitude, with students who were excluded for a fixed term taking a cue from their parents:

> As well as the teachers [it] depends on the parents and stuff because if you're excluded and you go home and your parents just don't, you know, care, and they let you sit in front of the telly and just sit there and doss and everything, you're just going to come back and say 'Oh I'm just back at the same place again, it doesn't matter if I get expelled'. . . . But if the parents are strict with their children at home, I think that'll influence them a lot. So I guess . . . it is important that the teachers make an effort but I think it's more important if the parents make an effort.
>
> (speaker in group interview)

Another student placed more responsibility on the individual student. While in this example she was referring to truancy, she suggests inappropriate behaviour sometimes occurs because students do not care about their own education:

> There's bullying . . . if they're getting bullied then they're like afraid to come to school. Or if they just don't care really. It can also be that they haven't got respect for their mum and dad, I

mean because I didn't show a lot of respect for mum and dad because I bunked and that.

(Kirsty, mainstream school, no exclusions)

The girls argued that there should be shared responsibility for educational success and problem solving at school, although the extent to which they located primary responsibility in themselves, their teachers or their parents varied considerably. They were, however, in agreement that all parties were likely to make a greater effort to avoid a disciplinary exclusion when parents and school are working in co-operation. They suggest that risk of exclusion in some form is increased when there is conflict between parents and school. Nevertheless, as we illustrated in chapter 4, the unwillingness or inability of some parents to support or challenge actions taken by the school cannot be explained simply in terms of parents not caring. In many cases they were frustrated by the way in which the school reacted, particularly the school's failure to consult with them. Additionally, some parents were unsure about how best to support their daughters.

Some girls were dubious about the effectiveness not just of exclusion but of a full range of sanctions such as 'concern slips', working in isolation and 'being on report'. They argued that a student's own desire to make some changes is more important than any externally imposed sanction. Daniela drew on her own experience to argue that the desire for change and the motivation to learn had to come from the individual student:

I don't know how that's meant to change anyone. If a child's being naughty, I don't think it's the school that can help. The child needs to help themselves. That's what I had to do. The school didn't help me. I helped myself. . . . I hardly used to do any homework at all. I used to still get good reports but I just never used to do any classwork and I regret it now with GCSEs coming on. I just want to come out of here with some good grades so I can go to college.

(Daniela, mainstream school, fixed-term exclusions)

Another student at the same school, who had received several fixed-term exclusions earlier in her school career, mainly for becoming involved in physical fights, also attributed her improved behaviour more to changes within herself than to external sanctions. She thought that she had become more mature, more controlled and less impulsive (and therefore less likely to get into physical fights) as she had moved through the school:

> I don't like fighting, it just happened sometimes . . . and now I'm just more interested in the schoolwork and stuff. I'm more mature than in the other years. I learned to control my temper and not to fight in school . . . I'd rather argue.
>
> (Tina)

These girls had found a way, however haphazard, of ensuring their ongoing inclusion in mainstream schools. We now look at the experiences of those who had not been as successful in negotiating the challenges and who consequently were excluded from their mainstream school, formally or otherwise, and were being educated in alternative settings. We suggest that their generally more positive experiences in pupil referral units, further education colleges, work experience placements and an 'in-school' centre highlight practices and approaches which can inform the development of more inclusive schools.

Inclusion through exclusion?

Those girls who were receiving alternative education generally had a very positive attitude towards that provision and appeared highly motivated, even though many were initially unsure about what to expect. This suggests that their previous behavioural difficulties can be explained, at least in part, in terms of institutional and structural factors (Lloyd and O'Regan, 1999; Pomeroy, 2000). Their accounts suggest that the curriculum was more closely matched to their needs and current competencies and that they were able to receive a higher degree of teacher support in comparison with students in much larger mainstream classes. Learning gaps could be filled and social, emotional and behavioural difficulties addressed. They also valued support in gathering information about post-compulsory schooling and training opportunities.

One Year 11 student, who had missed a considerable amount of schooling during Years 8 and 9, was reintroduced to Year 7 work in one particular subject when she began at a PRU. Rather than adopting a negative perspective on this, she valued the learning opportunity:

Yeah, like they gave me . . . they start off with work from Year 7 to bring you up to date with everything. I didn't mind because I knew I'd missed out on so much and I'd got a chance to catch up with it all now.

(Belinda, self-excluder)

She went on to explain how the low teacher–student ratio and high levels of support enabled her to maintain a positive attitude and high level of motivation:

Here, the groups are small. In my group there's only five people and the teacher's got more time to spend with us. Teachers explain the work. If we don't understand it, we stay behind and they'll go through it. One day I didn't understand some work and one of the teachers went through it *three* times with me, so I knew what to do, but in mainstream they just keep telling you what to do, give you your books and you've all got to do it. So if you don't do it, you don't do it.

(Belinda)

For another student it was the social, emotional and behavioural support that she received at a PRU that she found particularly useful. Opportunities to talk things through meant that she remained focused on her educational goals and gradually developed a greater repertoire of responses to other students' provocative behaviour. 'Having a temper' and 'being easily wound up' had previously been dominant features of Rachael's personality. Physical fights and verbal abuse, her two main responses to difficulties, had contributed in no small way to her permanent disciplinary exclusion. She was now determined that old patterns of behaviour did not continue to interfere with her education:

I haven't lost my temper properly since I've been here. It was in [a particular class with a particular teacher] and Ryan called me a silly bitch so I stood up and like started mouthing back and that. I knew [the teacher] was like coming in front of us so I didn't hit him [Ryan]. [The teacher] started talking to me and that, calmed me down . . . 'What's the matter?' and like stuff like that. That's why I think I'm still here. It's not worth it, do you know what I mean . . . it's not worth getting kicked out of school for it.

(Rachael, fixed-term and permanent exclusions)

While smaller classes often enable teachers and students to establish better working relationships, and may enable pressured teachers to give more time to individuals, different ways of speaking, listening and responding to students can also make a difference. Girls reported that 'being shouted at', for example, resulted in them not only feeling disrespected but also disrespecting the teacher who shouted. Rachael explained how the less formal nature of the PRU and the greater respect she was shown were important factors in her successful integration:

> I dunno. I think it's 'cause like you can call the teachers by their first name and like they respect you. They talk to you like you're on the same level as them . . . you're no less important or nothing. They treat you the same and like they don't shout at you. If you do something wrong they talk to you about it instead of mouthing off and shouting . . . which just makes pupils shout back.
>
> (Rachael)

Those students attending FE colleges on part-time placements expressed similar sentiments. Emma and Megan, both of whom had missed a considerable amount of schooling through non-attendance, reported attending their classes regularly. Emma's courses required attendance for four days a week and Megan's, three. They enjoyed the less formal nature of the college environment, such as calling tutors by their first name, as well as the more personal relationships with their tutors and the smaller class sizes (two teachers to twelve pupils). They talked about feeling as though they were treated in more respectful and 'grown-up' ways. Megan appreciated that there was a counsellor to whom she could talk and that there was no requirement to wear school uniform.

Developing more flexible arrangements, such as part-time work experience or FE college placements, is one way that some mainstream schools are attempting to meet the needs of students who are experiencing difficulties. Sam, a Year 11 student in a mainstream school who had been formally 'disapplied' from some parts of the National Curriculum, was spending two days a week on work experience at a beauty salon. She had chosen to limit her work experience to two days a week because she wanted more GCSEs and had found it too difficult to catch up with work missed while she was away on work experience. Despite this tension, she valued the placement, which had motivated her to secure a place in college:

> You can get two things out of the work experience. You get experience of the world of work, and maybe you get, like I've done, a job out of it. They've put me on a training package. I really want to get in at college as well. I need three GCSEs and I've got one.
>
> (Sam)

Sam's mother also supported the arrangement, reporting that Sam had established good working relationships and had gained self-confidence and self-esteem at the placement. Her attendance at school during the remaining three days had also improved considerably.

'In-school' centres are another way in which some mainstream schools are aiming to support students who are experiencing learning or behavioural difficulties and thereby reduce exclusions. Since students remain on-site, they can still take part in some parts of the curriculum with their classmates while at the same time receiving specialised learning and behaviour support in the centre, before being gradually reintegrated back into the mainstream. Jane was a Year 11 student who had joined the school at the end of Year 10 after having arrived from another part of the country where she had been permanently excluded. Prior to this, she had missed a considerable amount of schooling through truancy. She experienced difficulties managing the work in many of her subjects and had also exhibited challenging behaviour. She was enrolled for five GCSE examinations and during her free periods went to the school's in-school centre, known as the education support unit. She particularly valued the additional learning support she received in this unit and the opportunity to talk freely with a trusted adult about matters of concern to her, both in and out of school.

While the girls were clearly benefiting from alternative provision in PRUs, colleges and work placements, these arrangements were often far from ideal. As noted above, dual enrolment at a mainstream school alongside an FE college or work experience poses some problems with regard to catching up on missed classes. PRU staff also noted the limited facilities and smaller staff numbers meant that the range of GCSE subjects was limited and some students regretted not having access to a full range of options such as are available in mainstream schools. At the time of our interviews all the PRU provision we visited was part-time, and service providers noted this as a disadvantage.

Identifying good teachers

For girls in both mainstream schools and alternative settings, there was considerable consistency in how they defined and characterised a good teacher. There was also great variation in the attitudes which individual girls had towards different teachers and in the quality of the relationships that they had built with them. When relationships were poor or when a teacher was judged not to respect students, this often had a direct impact on learning:

> I used to hate maths way up to Year 10 because we had a really bad maths teacher. He wouldn't make you work or anything and then they moved me to my new maths class and that attitude of the teacher is you do it or you get out. She's known to be really strict, but she's fair as well. And then there's some teachers, I don't know how to describe it, they always have to be right and even when they're not they try and make out as if they are.
>
> (Frances, mainstream school, no exclusions)

In the girls' view, good teachers were those who were competent in their subject knowledge, had good classroom management skills and were able to establish mutually respectful and trusting relationships with students. This included being flexible in their approach to teaching, strict but relaxed (being able to 'have a laugh') and having high expectations of students. Cheryl and Michelle explained how teachers who were 'lax' were viewed as incompetent and lacking in concern about the educational progress of their students:

Cheryl: Although it sounds really weird, we enjoy lessons with teachers who are strict more than with teachers who are really lax. It's productive.

Michelle: Yeah it's really weird. My maths teacher is really strict and I really enjoy her lessons. With [another teacher] it's just like a free for all and no one likes going because it's fall asleep in her lesson and everything. She just doesn't care.

Fairness and consistency were highly valued attributes and were

regarded as critical when a teacher was investigating an alleged mis-
demeanour. The girls argued it was important that a teacher ascer-
tained all sides of a story, including looking beyond the immediate
behaviour to some of the underlying causes. It was important that
they did not privilege another teacher's perspective over that of a
student and, when appropriate, that they applied sanctions consistently. Students stressed the importance of feeling listened to and
regarded it as unfair if teachers talked casually and publicly about
misbehaviour:

> The teachers are listening to the teachers and not the pupils.
>
> (speaker in group interview, PRU)

> Or say I've misbehaved in a lesson with one teacher, they'll go to
> the staffroom [and talk] . . . and it's like they'll think I'm like
> that with all teachers.
>
> (speaker in group interview, mainstream school)

Some students found themselves in disagreement with certain
school rules. They expressed frustration about rules such as being
forced to go outside in wet and cold weather, and felt it was unfair
that there was little apparent flexibility or opportunity to review
such rules.

Students associated consistency with equal treatment for all. They
noted any kind of bias, whether based on race, gender or individual
difference. Two students in a mainstream school provided an
example of inconsistency in their form teacher's apparent tolerance
of certain 'loud' students:

Nicole: Like for example our form teacher . . . there's two people in
the class, a boy and a girl, they are both really loud but because
that behaviour is expected of them, they can get away with it.
She just ignores them but every time someone else does it they
get punished.

Kim: It's unfair because they should be treated equally. The teachers
always go on about we need to handle our responsibilities and
our rights but we can't do that if we've got someone else shouting across the classroom. That doesn't set an example for us, if
they get away with it.

They also argued that consistent standards should be applied in
relation to homework:

Homework . . . 'cause if some people don't bring it in and they say 'Oh give it to me on Monday', and Monday comes, 'Oh give it to me on Wednesday'. And then I might have brought mine in last week and spent loads of time doing it for it to be in that day and he doesn't really care.

(Nicole, mainstream school, no exclusions)

Any perceived double standard was likely to engender feelings of resentment. A strong theme running though their discussions was the need for more equal and mutually respectful relationships with teachers:

I hate it when teachers can embarrass you in front of the class, but if you embarrass them . . . it's like different.

(Dianne, mainstream school, no exclusions)

Teaching competence featured strongly in the girls' discussions. They regarded it as important that a teacher was able to pitch lesson content at the right level and to provide extra help when needed. Work that was too easy was usually considered boring, while work that was too hard became discouraging. Both engender frustration and have a detrimental effect on student motivation:

I put my hand up and she's like 'I'll be with you in a minute' and if I kept my hand up I'd sit there with my hand up for over half an hour.

(Joanne, mainstream school, internal and fixed-term exclusions)

Planning lessons which have sufficient flexibility and differentiation to cater for the wide range of interests and abilities found within any class is a considerable challenge for any teacher, as is being able to provide the necessary learning support, given the size of most mainstream classes. One response is to use a range of pedagogies, in which students are encouraged, or at least allowed, to support each other's learning through group work and other co-operative activities. A number of students were frustrated that mutual support and co-operation were discouraged, particularly when the teacher appeared too hard-pressed to provide direct support:

You can't understand the work so you ask your friend rather

than ask the teacher because normally they say hold on about 20 minutes, so you ask your friend next to you and they try helping you and you get told off for it and sent out. That's just bad luck if you get caught like that.

(Julie, mainstream school, no exclusions)

In the example above, the student appears to be resigned to the situation, yet teacher reluctance to allow co-operation may affect girls disproportionately. There is evidence to suggest that while boys tend to dominate teacher attention, girls rely more heavily on their female peers for help (Kelly, 1988; Howe, 1997; Hey et al., 1998). Service providers in our study also observed that girls have closer social networks and are more likely to support each other's learning than are boys.

The girls considered praise and encouragement from teachers to be important for motivation and confidence building. Heaviest condemnation was reserved for teachers who engaged in student put-downs:

When teachers put you down, you just don't stretch . . . and if they're not stretching you, you won't know if you can do it. My German teacher is really good. He's like 'I know you can do this, I know you can do this' and that's what you need . . . encouragement. The difference is our maths teacher. She's like 'Quite frankly you'll do crap'. And anyone you ask will say she's a shitty teacher.

(speaker in group interview)

However, as pointed out by a speaker in that same group interview, praise is only valued when it is credible:

In my maths group I don't do any work. Like the whole hour lesson I just spend messing around with Chrissie and that . . . I don't like maths anyway . . . and I'll do like one question then I'm fooling around and I get sent outside. Then I come back in and I'm sent outside again and at the end of the day she's like: 'Well done Michelle, you're doing much better'.

Favourite and least favourite subjects appeared to be related more closely to the teacher than the subject content. Teacher expectation as well as the efforts teachers put into their lessons influenced girls' attitude to their schoolwork, as did structural factors such as the use of sets (grouping students by ability).

Students' proposals for change

The girls had a range of suggestions about how schools might be improved. We have already noted the importance which students placed on good relationships with teachers, placing particular emphasis on open communication, respect and teacher care. Structural and organisational issues also featured prominently in their discussions. They argued for smaller classes and reflected on the negative impact which ability grouping arrangements such as sets had on some students. They believed it important that schools have a school council (or a more effective school council) to encourage student participation in school decision-making. They saw the need for schools to appoint a student counsellor and to provide students in difficulties with a range of sources of help. They advocated more parental involvement and a greater emphasis on preventing bullying. The curriculum was targeted as a potential site for change, particularly in relation to diversity and multiculturalism.

Girls only space

Some girls thought that having some 'girls only' space would be helpful, whether this be physical space, such as a designated time for exclusive access to the gym or a forum where they could discuss issues that relate mainly to girls. With regard to sport, the girls in one group interview argued that more needed to be done to encourage greater participation among girls. One of the greatest difficulties was in the attitude that boys displayed towards girls' bodies:

S1:   I know that I don't particularly play the sport, but I know that some girls would like to have a girls' football team.

S2:   Yeah, I think there's a lot of sexism involved in school because like, you know, it's boys' basketball team, boys' football team. Where do the girls come into all this?

S3:   Fitness I think would have to be separate. You know when you go into the fitness weight rooms . . . and some of the girls are bigger than others, they [boys] just laugh at their bodies and things. So I think that's one thing they should be separated in.

(group interview, mainstream school)

Tackling bullying

Students at some schools wanted their school to take a more pro-active approach in tackling bullying. Some suggestions, such as having more teachers around during breaks, imply that bullying can be addressed through 'policing' by teachers. This type of approach may sometimes be necessary, but, as other girls implied, it serves to address a symptom rather than underlying causes of a deeper problem. Students acknowledged that changing the school culture would be a more effective strategy and would contribute to a more productive learning environment but that it requires a long-term sustained approach and not merely cosmetic change:

SI: They tried to change things. They've got these signs up saying that you've entered a bully-free zone but it doesn't happen. Bullying still goes on in school.

S2:   And it can affect their schoolwork as well . . . 'cause it's distracting them from their work, so they're not getting good grades . . .

(group interview, mainstream school)

Another group of girls discussed the possibility of challenging various forms of bullying through the curriculum. The girls drew attention to the importance of schools being proactive in promoting tolerance and celebrating diversity. One explained how coverage of concepts such as discrimination and racism, including reading about and discussing the Stephen Lawrence case helped address racial harassment and bullying:

At school we did a project a while back about racism in the community and everything, so I think that has helped to educate quite a lot of people.

(Michelle, mainstream school)

The curriculum

Students and parents at one school serving a diverse community in a large multicultural city felt that the curriculum did not address their everyday realities. They perceived the curriculum to be narrow and largely monocultural, thus serving as an inadequate preparation for life. Issues of ethnicity and racism were avoided or covered by chance or in a haphazard way. Such issues were raised by white students as well as those from minority communities, but among mothers, the only white women to raise the issue were parents of mixed heritage children.

> Pupils should be taught more about other cultures. There are many other cultures . . . and some [students] don't realise [that] . . . and they come out not knowing anything about other cultures.
>
> (Daniela's mother)

Some girls suggested that curriculum coverage of topics such as racism, religious and cultural diversity and sexuality were avoided because they were too sensitive or controversial. Dianne, a Year 11 student of African Caribbean heritage, identified Religious Education and English as two subjects in which she recalled some curriculum coverage of racial and cultural issues. She felt this coverage had been minimal and implied that in the resulting discussion racist and anti-democratic sentiments had been given free expression:

> You do a little bit here and there but not much. Maybe that's for the best. So many different things come out and arguments and debates happen in class and all that sort of stuff and people do get offended with that because there's so many varied opinions.
>
> (Dianne, mainstream school)

Girls and parents also expressed concern over the way in which academic achievements, as measured by examinations, are privileged over other forms of achievement and the way in which this results in some students coming to view themselves as failures. A number of researchers have drawn links between disaffection and an overly prescriptive curriculum (Hatcher, 1998; Munn et al., 2000), while others have advocated a broader approach, with due attention being given to important but non-examinable subjects such as Personal, Social and Health Education (Thacker et al., 2002). Several parents spoke positively about the way in which work experience and vocational courses had resulted in improved motivation and confidence for their daughters.

Parental involvement

Both girls and their parents identified greater parental involvement and better communication between home and school as critical in ensuring the continued engagement and motivation of students. Several girls who had been excluded from mainstream education thought it would have been better if their parents had known sooner about their difficulties in school. Rachael, who was being educated in a PRU, thought that her former school, in placing responsibility on her to deliver the school's letters to her mother about fixed-term exclusions, was not selecting an effective channel of communication. After the first few exclusions, Rachael chose not to deliver subsequent letters and instead would spend the day on the streets or at a friend's house while leading her mother to believe that she was attending school. Rachael suggested that parents should be informed when there are positive reports on a student, as well as problems. Her comments highlight the impact of this particular strategy:

> Involve the parents more . . . 'cause I didn't really want my mum to know what I was like at school. If they involve the parents more . . . like here, if you are good they phone your mum and mum gets really chuffed when they phone her and tell her how good I've been . . . and that makes me happy 'cause my mum's happy . . . and like it's different.
>
> (Rachael)

Sources of support

Many of the girls talked about the potential usefulness of a school counsellor and some reported using the school nurse or education welfare officer as someone in whom they could confide problems. A number argued that students needed to have direct access to this sort of support:

> I think we should have a school counsellor. As teenagers we go through a lot of stuff . . . we've got troubles at home, we've got troubles at school, you've got to fit in or whatever and it would just be nice if there was someone you could talk to about it.
>
> (Cheryl, mainstream school, internal exclusions)

In a group discussion, one student suggested that girls tend to find it easier to talk to a female counsellor, whereas for boys either a man or woman was likely to be equally approachable:

> It's true boys don't have problems going to a woman . . . you know a female teacher and talking about their problems . . . but I think a lot of girls do have a problem going to male though.
>
> (speaker in group interview)

Some students also suggested that teachers as well as students needed a range of strategies when a student was in danger of losing their temper or getting 'wound up'. Rachael, who was attending a PRU, suggested that for her, greater flexibility in how teachers responded to her would have been helpful. She clearly wanted to avoid getting into a 'rowing match' with her teachers, a desire that was almost certainly reciprocated by her teachers:

> Say like . . . say something happened in your lesson and you don't want to mouth off at the teacher . . . so if you could like walk out into a room somewhere where you could sit to calm down or something, just calm yourself down and then go back to your lesson, that's what I would have found helpful. 'Cause what I used to do was just walk out of the classroom and then I'd get done for walking out of the classroom. But I'd prefer that rather than have a rowing match with the teacher or something.
>
> (Rachael)

The advantages and limitations of 'time-out', whether self-imposed or teacher directed, are open to debate. Rachael's comments suggest the potential for a dialogue and a negotiation that would have served the purposes of both teacher and student. Brief periods of student-chosen 'time-out', for example, could have formed part of a wider intervention aimed at addressing Rachael's emotional and behavioural difficulties. If teachers are able to respond in the ways Rachael implies, and has since experienced in the PRU, there are considerable implications for teacher training and development.

In line with this, other girls asked that schools do more to understand and address girls' difficulties, including listening more to students:

Like, try and work it out or see what's gone wrong before you
actually suspend someone.

(Tina, fixed-term exclusion)

The critical importance of listening to students and effectively
addressing their concerns, considering all sides of a story, valuing
student perspectives and addressing social and emotional needs have
been highlighted in previous research, including our own (Pomeroy,
2000; Cooper *et al.*, 2000; Osler, 2000). Some girls drew attention to
the value of effective school councils as one way in which students'
needs can be addressed and young people can have a say in decision-
making and management of their school:

I think the absence of the school council lately has caused a bit
of . . . I mean you want to talk to people. I know people who
wanted lockers for five years in the school and have not been
able to get anywhere near because of the school council.

(speaker in group interview)

The value and challenges of ensuring students voices are being
heard through mechanisms such as a school council have been discussed by researchers and practitioners (Cunningham, 1991,
2000; Osler and Starkey, 1996; Thorne, 1996; Osler, 2000). A number of these accounts stress how effective school councils help
schools to meet the obligation to consider young people's opinions
in matters or procedures affecting them, in line with article 12 of the
UN Convention on the Rights of the Child.

Flexible pastoral support strategies, where teachers as well as
students are actively involved in resolving the issues that affect
them, were considered to be helpful by the girls. Opportunities
for promoting involvement in school decision-making develop
valuable communication skills but have also been found to have a
positive impact on student behaviour and motivation (Osler,
2000). Both parents and students saw the high staff turnover
rates in some schools as extremely problematic, impacting negatively on student motivation and well-being. The use of supply
teachers was viewed as detrimental to the learning of some
students:

They've gone through quite a few supply teachers and I don't
think that's helped. It kind of makes them unstable doesn't

it? I mean with people coming and going all the time, it's hard.

(Tina's mother)

The use of sets

In all the schools we visited the practice of setting was used to group students according to their perceived ability. Also in operation was a tiered exam system (see chapter 2), whereby certain students were entered for examinations in which the best grade they could achieve was less than a C, the lowest grade considered to be a good grade. This restricted their access to certain training opportunities, advanced academic study and thus to higher education.

Girls expressed reservations about the use of sets. They thought, for example, that some students in lower sets are capable of more but do not get the chance to sit the higher paper. One group explained that test results are used to decide who gets placed in which set but that teachers also wish to keep particular individuals apart. One girl thought that she was in a lower set than she should be because of her behaviour rather than her ability. There was also a feeling among some of those in lower sets that the teachers had given up on them in terms of examination success. This undermined their confidence and motivation. As one participant put it:

> I didn't revise. None of my friends that are in the lowest group ever revise. You can't be bothered. If you're told that you're crap, you're going to act like you're crap.
>
> (speaker in group interview, mainstream school)

Some girls commented on the expectations that are placed on those in higher sets to move quickly and easily through the curriculum. Others spoke of unequal treatment between the different sets. The girls in one group interview could not agree on which set gets more 'privileges' but perceived teachers generally to be more concerned about the performance of those in higher sets:

S1:   Set one's get more privileges than the other sets 'cause they're clever, so they take more notice of them.

S2:   People in set one get loads of stuff, people in set four or five get loads of stuff and people in the middle get nothing.

S1:   Like in maths, we do like Year 8 work.

S3: It's just that I think the people in set three, which is average, actually get more privileges as well . . . cause they get to do their tests early . . . and they're [the teachers] always concentrating on the set ones, not bothering about us.

(group interview, mainstream school)

In a system that places high value on A–C examination grades it is not surprising that those who are viewed as unlikely to reach that target experience a 'second-class version of success' (Benjamin, 2000) and see the system as failing them. The girls' comments are reflected in recent research which found that students in lower sets reported loss of motivation when they realised their teachers were preparing them for examinations that gave access to only the lowest grades, while some of those in higher sets, particularly the girls, experienced anxiety because of high expectations, fast-paced lessons and pressure to succeed. For students in both of these groups, achievement was lower than what was expected given their level of attainment in school entry tests (Boaler *et al.*, 2000). The researchers also found that social class had influenced teacher decisions on which students were allocated to particular sets, with a dis-proportionate number of working-class students being allocated to low sets.

The girls in our study were generally sceptical about the use of exclusion as a disciplinary sanction and shared the perception of a number of the professionals that it is used somewhat inconsistently both within and between schools. Those who had been excluded or who had effectively self-excluded and were being educated in alter-native provision, often experienced these alternatives more posi-tively. In particular they valued the individual support and better quality relationships with teachers. They recognised, however, that curriculum options and choices were often more restricted and that there were practical difficulties in combining school with training or a college placement. Whether or not individuals had experienced alternatives to school, they showed considerable insight and clarity in identifying what makes schools inclusive and were able to make a number of concrete recommendations. Their recommendations covered both interpersonal relationships and organisational issues.

Chapter 6

Barriers to achievement

This chapter examines the barriers to achievement that girls face. It draws on the perspectives of professionals as well as a range of perspectives from girls themselves. We examine the links between informal and formal exclusion, truancy and absenteeism. We focus on aspirations, caring responsibilities, pregnancy, sexual vulnerability and peer relationships. Service providers highlight girls' limited access to support systems and argue that while these meet the needs of some girls, they fail to address the needs of others. We argue that unless we identify the varied but specific needs of girls, policies and practices which attempt to reduce school exclusion, truancy and disaffection are unlikely to have a significant impact on the wider problem of social exclusion.

School absenteeism

Both researchers and policy-makers link truancy with school exclusion, juvenile crime and an increased likelihood of becoming a teenage parent. Truancy is also associated with negative outcomes such as later unemployment, homelessness and poor mental and physical health (SEU, 1998; Reid, 1999). As we note in chapter 4, all but one of the girls in our study reported truanting for brief periods of time. A smaller but significant number reported missing extended periods of school and eight girls had ceased attending their mainstream school altogether. Thus, truancy among girls appears to be more widespread than is sometimes acknowledged.

The service providers we interviewed consistently identified absenteeism, including complete withdrawal from school, as a concern which affects girls disproportionately, and as something which has a negative impact on their educational and life chances. This is unsurprising given that many of the other concerns which professionals raised about girls (caring responsibilities, problematic relationships with peers, pregnancy, low aspirations, sexual exploitation) tend to manifest themselves through non-attendance.

Many service providers expressed the view that more girls than boys self-exclude, attributing this, in part, to differences in girls' and boys' responses to difficulties at school and at home. While acknowledging that he was generalising, and that he had worked with girls who were confrontational and aggressive, one deputy headteacher felt that gendered responses to stressful home circumstances resulted in girls being more vulnerable to self-exclusion, in contrast to their male peers whose behaviour was likely to lead directly to disciplinary exclusion:

> There are those kids who are in very difficult circumstances outside of school and therefore bring a whole load of baggage in to school which makes the probability of them surviving their statutory school years less likely. The boys are more likely to present that maybe with aggression, which makes it inevitable for short-term exclusion and the girls, frankly, will just stop coming before that . . . or will find other ways of dealing with it.
>
> (deputy head)

Another interviewee also argued that schools' failure to meet girls' needs led them to drop out rather than draw attention to themselves through aggressive behaviour:

> It's their response to a school that is not accommodating them . . . instead of acting out.
>
> (educational psychologist)

These views confirm girls' own assessments that self-exclusion is a coping strategy more likely to be employed by girls than boys. A Year 11 student suggested that in her experience truanting, particularly longer-term truanting, was more prevalent among girls:

> A little bit it does seem to me like it's more girls. You also get quite a few boys bunking but the ones that I know who've been bunking a long period of time, it's girls.
>
> (Kirsty, mainstream school)

Behaviour support staff in one LEA reported that the students referred to them for attendance difficulties were predominantly girls. The head of a pupil referral unit (PRU) argued that, in her experience, students referred to the provision as school-refusers had similar needs to those referred because they had been permanently excluded. In other words, the students experienced similar difficulties in schools but responded to them differently. Most of the school refusers were girls:

> The boys that come here on the whole don't want to be excluded . . . they want to be at school and they attend well here. At the centre it's more girls that have been school refusers and they are more likely to have attendance problems at the centre.
>
> (head of PRU)

Service providers recognised that the reasons for non-attendance are complex and varied and that the various factors are likely to interact in different ways for different students. School-based difficulties, out-of-school stress, parental and peer influences, individual characteristics and circumstances (for example, low self-esteem or aspirations, caring responsibilities) and school systems that are ineffective in responding to truancy were all seen as contributing to poor attendance. Truancy was generally acknowledged to be a complex, multidimensional problem:

> Some of the ones I get referred to me, it is the result of something like bullying but it's too simple to say that it is just to do with bullying. It could be to do with confidence, self-esteem, all those sorts of things. Girls often fall in and out of friendships and stuff like that. Or there could be one too many stresses in the young person's life.
>
> (educational psychologist)

The head of another PRU suggested that absenteeism generally reflected difficulties coping with the structure, organisation and management of mainstream schools. She confirmed the views of girls in this study who argue that class size, complex organisational arrangements and difficulties in establishing good relationships with staff and peers all contribute to the problem. She also suggested that the inflexible nature of school systems and curriculum arrangements mean that they are unable to meet the needs of a diverse school population. She suggests that for some students this inevitably leads to alienation:

> It's about [lack of] diversity of provision. You either go to a homogeneous mainstream school and you're shoehorned into that, and if you can't do that then you're special and you go off to special school.
>
> (head of PRU)

She noted how some 'disaffected' students flourish in an alternative environment such as a PRU, suggesting that for some students inclusion means being included (and educated) somewhere else. Citing the example of a student who had completely dropped out from her mainstream school yet had a 100 per cent attendance at the PRU, she concluded: 'She is not someone that didn't want to be educated'. While recognising that PRUs are not ideal, she argued that mainstream schools not only required major changes in their organisation and management, but that many also needed to adopt a radically different set of values. Her perspective was pragmatic, if somewhat pessimistic:

> It's going to take a long time, if ever, for schools to get where they need to be in order for all kids to be included.
>
> (head of PRU)

Parentally condoned absence

In some cases, service providers suggested that absenteeism was condoned by parents and often linked to caring responsibilities. Girls were seen as much more likely to engage in parentally condoned absence than boys. Some schools were thought to collude in the parentally condoned absence of girls:

> There are some issues around one of the secondary schools I cover where [there is a belief among some parents that] girls should be at home and then if there are any problems at home then they are there to help mum sort it out . . . Or they are just kept off school and that seems perfectly acceptable by the parents. . . . And the schools don't pick up on it.
>
> (educational psychologist)

The issue of parentally condoned truancy was also broached by the girls in our study. One group suggested that some parents 'do not seem to mind' if their children take time off school. One student argued that parents have a responsibility for their children's attendance, but not all took this seriously:

> Yeah, let their kids do that [take time off school]. 'Cause my mum wouldn't let me 'cause she thinks education is important. But some of them just say: 'Well it's up to you if you're never there'.
>
> (Nicole, mainstream school)

Some professionals thought that this approach was more common among parents who had themselves experienced little success or enjoyment at school:

> You get the parent who says, 'I didn't go to school. Look at me, I'm all right'.
>
> (education welfare officer)

Some service providers felt that lack of family support and encouragement has a direct and detrimental effect on both the aspirations and attendance of some girls. Again it was felt that girls are more likely than boys to be drawn into domestic duties, sometimes because their education was seen as less important than that of their brothers:

> In some families, education isn't valued. There are quite a few young women at home and they are helping with the cooking and the shopping. They don't see it [education] as a way to improve their life situations.
>
> (education welfare officer)

> I think there is still, even now, a tendency to see education as not as important for girls as it is for boys.
>
> (educational psychologist)

Two specific points at which service providers perceive students to be particularly vulnerable to self-exclusion are the transition from primary to secondary school and during the final year (Year 11) of compulsory schooling.

Addressing students' needs

In one secondary school an additional education welfare officer's post had been funded from various grants to supplement the education welfare services normally available. This extra resource meant that the school was able to focus on some of the needs it had been aware of but had been unable to address. This officer acknowledged the complex contexts in which she worked, and spoke of 'the presenting problem not always being the underlying problem'. She provided two examples. The first involved a girl whose attendance and behaviour had been a cause of concern. The education welfare officer's investigations brought to light the difficulties that this student was having coping with an alcoholic mother who was periodically trying to overdose. Her work also uncovered the student's own self-harming behaviour. As the officer pointed out, any attempt to address the absenteeism which failed to take into account the wider picture was unlikely to result in improved attendance. In a second example, the school had made special arrangements for a girl who was not attending because she was afraid that her mother, who was seriously ill, might die before she returned home from school. The school ensured that the student could phone or visit her mother at set times during the day, so enabling her to return to school.

This education welfare officer also suggested a link between truancy and exclusion. She argued that a narrow focus on attendance without addressing a student's underlying difficulties can sometimes lead, more or less directly, to disciplinary exclusion:

> Some will take two or three days off a week just to ease the pressure because they are not coping. If we deal with attendance in isolation then we are forcing those kids back into that situation five days a week. That's when it becomes too much for staff and pupils and a likely outcome is exclusion. For some, as attendance has improved, their behaviour has got worse.
>
> (education welfare officer)

Other service providers perceived a link between truancy and informal exclusion, suggesting that the non-attendance of a 'problem' student is sometimes seen as a welcome respite for the school. In some cases, this leads to school-condoned truancy. Others thought that the less overt and 'invisible' behaviour of some girls causes them to fall through the net of support systems. Girls may opt out in a way that does not draw attention to them. Some schools, by failing to take action, or even by removing absent students from the school roll, effectively permit such students to drop out of school:

> These girls are very good at disappearing because they disappear quietly . . . they are not troublemakers, they are 'opters out'.
> (co-ordinator of multi-agency support)

> Some girls basically just drop out and don't question what their rights are . . . or you get a school where they say, you're not attending so we'll take you off the school roll. You can see how it's easy to opt out at any time.
> (manager of special project)

Some schools on the other hand invest considerable resources in attempting to follow up truancy but still feel they are making little progress with some girls. For a minority of students neither the school nor their families may be in a position to intervene:

> When I'm talking about girls disappearing from the scene, I mean five or six currently in Year 11, maybe another few in Year 10 who . . . we're back to that condoned absence and things like that. . . . But I mean there are one or two of those girls who are no longer living at home and seemingly home can't tell us where they are . . . you know?
> (deputy headteacher, large mainstream school)

During Year 11 schools may be reluctant to invest scarce resources in students who are approaching the end of their statutory school years. At this stage in particular, non-attending girls may be overlooked in favour of students (typically boys) who are engaging in overtly disruptive behaviour and thus threatening other students' learning:

> Students who are coming up to the end of their education and are disaffected . . . perhaps their attendance drops. These students are less likely to have anyone do anything for them and are more likely to get lost to the systems. I think there are quite a lot of girls in that category.
> (education welfare officer)

School attempts to monitor truancy, for example by having a 'first-day contact' policy, are unlikely to be effective if they lack the resources to implement the policy. As the girls at one school pointed out, students are adept at finding and exploiting the weaknesses in any system. Once they were aware that not all absences were followed up with a phone-call to parents, the new strategy lost much of its deterrent power.

The girls' reports suggested that 'policing' practices such as strategically placed CCTV cameras and a policy of 'first-day contact' when implemented consistently may be effective in reducing truancy among some students. Such measures, however, do little to address the underlying question, that of transforming schools to become inclusive institutions. The deeper challenge is to create a sense of belonging and to enable students to feel respected and valued participants in the processes of learning and teaching.

Re-integration

Both girls and professionals noted the difficulties that can arise when a student returns to school after an absence. Many professionals stressed how anything (truancy, illness, fixed-term exclusion, a change of school) that prevents a student attending school, even for a short period, can increase the likelihood of future non-attendance. Some argued that even sporadic truancy can undermine a student's opportunities to form positive relationships with peers and teachers and reduce their likelihood of keeping up with curriculum content. Particular concern was expressed about students who miss extended periods of school, with several professionals suggesting that re-integration support is often limited or non-existent. For some students, re-establishing a regular routine of attendance after an extended absence is a major challenge which must be faced alongside other challenges such as filling learning gaps and re-establishing other interpersonal and academic skills and habits. For long-term truants:

> Not being able to do the work and not getting the support needed to succeed [can be a problem] and school can be a very difficult place for them to be. They have to conform to certain expectations, which is hard for them if they have not been to school for too long. If you haven't done French for several years, it is very difficult to get back into doing it.
>
> (head of support service for children in public care)

Reports from both girls and professionals about truancy, self-exclusion and other avoidance strategies suggest that the official statistics concerning truancy under-represent the extent of this problem among girls. Non-attendance is more easily overlooked than more overtly disruptive behaviours, typically practised by boys. Nevertheless, it has a detrimental impact on the achievement and future life chances of many girls.

Informal exclusion

Informal, unofficial exclusion, whereby schools ask a student to stay away for a few days, or suggest to parents that they find an alternative school for their child, is a common and growing problem which is sometimes underestimated by local authorities (Lloyd, 2000; Osler *et al.*, 2000).

> They have called my mum into school and said Nadine's going to have to take a couple of days off school because she did such 'n such . . . and then I'd have to go home and then I'm not allowed back in school for about three or four days.
>
> (Nadine, PRU)

> It is hard to get schools to co-operate fully and for us to be able to scrutinise what they are recording [with regard to exclusion and truancy]. And there are a lot of informal exclusions going on.
>
> (senior LEA officer)

In this study, service providers and parents expressed concern about a range of school practices that result directly or indirectly in informal exclusion, whether this be exclusion from individual lessons, specific areas of the curriculum or more generally from school. Reported examples of the latter included asking students to 'stay at home for a few days' and suggestions that a student does not return to school the following academic year. As we have seen, some schools simply do not take the action required to enable and support vulnerable young people in school, while others may simply remove a non-attender from the school roll. There may sometimes be a fine line between informal exclusion and self-exclusion:

> One of the girls we're working with at the moment . . . she's not

> formally excluded but she's definitely been nudged out. Some
> of them actually leave before they are excluded.
>
> (youth worker)

Similarly, an education welfare officer suggested that in some cases,
schools may fail to refer a student to the education welfare service
because they do not want that student to return to school. He
identified this as another form of unofficial exclusion.

Pregnancy is one means by which some girls become more vulnerable to informal exclusion. The manager of a teenage pregnancy
project reported several cases of school insurance being used as an
excuse for informally excluding pregnant teenagers. This is despite
official policy which specifies that pregnancy is not a reason for
exclusion. The manager of a different project recounted the experiences of two pregnant schoolgirls with whom she had worked.
Neither had been in school for some years. They had not been formally excluded but had been removed from the school roll:

> I think the attitude was, 'you're not attending, this isn't working
> out but we're not going to exclude you, so we'll take you off the
> school roll 'cause you're not attending'.
>
> (manager of project for disaffected young people)

She argued that this conveys the message: 'If you drop out of the
system, you are not our responsibility any more'. In another
example, a parent, while acknowledging the difficulties presented by
her daughter at school, perceived the school as having given up on
her daughter and as actively discouraging her from returning to
school:

> And she [teacher responsible for pastoral support] more or less
> said, both to me and to Joanne, 'Don't bother coming back'.

Joanne's mother believed that earlier and more consistent intervention, including better communication with home, may have
prevented the extent of the relationship breakdown between her
daughter and certain teachers. In this case, the parent was concerned
about her daughter's increasing non-attendance but felt powerless to
insist that she attend a school where she was clearly not welcome.

The girls also provided examples of informal exclusion. Caroline
had effectively been excluded from her previous school, following a

period of poor attendance. Her account conveyed a strong sense of rejection concerning this informal exclusion. She did not begin school again until six months later when her family moved to another city:

> Like in Year 9 I didn't go that much. I'd just basically bunked nearly the whole year . . . so they just said, there's no point in you coming back in Year 10. They didn't even write a letter to my mum, they just kept on hinting to me, saying 'Caroline, there's no point in you coming to school. You don't learn, you don't do anything, so you might as well not come to this school any more'.
>
> (Caroline, mainstream school)

Interestingly, Caroline had not truanted since starting at her new school. She attributed this to a change within herself and coming to realise that she really did want 'an education':

> You don't realise what you're missing out on until you actually bunk that long. I don't bunk at all no more 'cause I realised that I missed out on too much and I'm not going to get anywhere if I keep on bunking and that.
>
> (Caroline)

It is likely that other factors such as a different peer group (and possibly a different peer culture with regard to attendance) and the opportunity to develop more constructive relationships with the teachers at the new school also contributed to Caroline's changed attitude. Despite having missed so much school that it was difficult to keep up in some classes, she appeared determined to persevere and to seek help where needed.

The main concerns expressed in relation to informal exclusion were, first, the ease with which some pupils can 'opt out' or be 'nudged out' of the system and, second, the way in which this undermines parental and student rights to be involved in decision-making. Third, informal exclusion means that schools are not accountable in any way to the local authority, and there is no opportunity to question the appropriateness of actions taken. There are both legal and ethical implications. The lack of recording and monitoring of informal exclusions means that these practices disguise further the amount of school being missed by certain pupils.

Caring responsibilities

Many service providers identified caring responsibilities as a major barrier restricting girls' access and participation in education. A number viewed young carers as a neglected group whose particular educational needs were often overlooked.

> This girl's a school refuser ... and she's a school refuser because her mother is terminally ill and she's doing a lot of the caring.
>
> (member of LEA behaviour support team)

The term 'caring responsibilities' appeared to cover a broad range of activities and was used to refer to the care of an older family member (parent, grandparent) and young children. Service providers made reference to regular domestic chores such as preparing meals, cleaning, minding younger siblings, and grocery shopping as well as to the special responsibilities placed on children who were providing physical care to a parent with a disability, poor mental health, a medical condition or drug or alcohol dependency. Many interviewees stressed that both boys and girls act as carers but perceived that girls are more likely to take on such responsibilities:.

> I think girls are much more likely to be put under pressure to become carers, one way or another, with siblings or for parents ... so there is a domestic pressure and absences and non-attendance will be down on their record.
>
> (alternative education co-ordinator)

One of the main concerns was the impact caring responsibilities can have on school attendance and late arrival at school. One participant drew attention to a Children's Society study on young carers (Frank *et al.*, 1999) which showed that on average the attendance of young carers was as high as that of other pupils. Most of the participants in that study were caring for an ill parent. He thought it important to distinguish these young carers from those that are kept home to look after younger siblings or to undertake domestic chores where lateness and non-attendance do become a significant problem. Once established, certain roles and patterns of behaviour can be difficult to change:

> Because they've not been in school for some time, they've got into this role and parents are very reluctant to take them out of it.
>
> (head of PRU)

For some girls, there is a close link between caring and self-exclusion:

> Then they move into a sort of self-excluding scenario because they are falling back in their schoolwork and other things in their lives are assuming more importance.
>
> (alternative education co-ordinator)

One of the girls we interviewed revealed that she had missed a significant amount of primary school because of caring for her grandmother. Both the school and social services attempted to address the problem, but not in ways that proved to be helpful. Following warnings that she would not be allowed to go on living with her grandmother, she promised to improve her attendance:

> I was living with my natural nan at the time and she used to get really ill, so I wouldn't go in because I'd look after her. At the school they said: 'Look, if you carry on doing this you're going to have to move away from your nan because you're not allowed to stay off school to look after her at your age'. But I just stopped going and stayed home.
>
> (Stephanie, FE college)

Stephanie later began to self-exclude and went on to miss a considerable amount of her secondary schooling before eventually being enrolled in an under-16s course at an FE college.

For some young carers, even when attendance was good, anxiety about a parent with a medical or other condition was seen as having a detrimental effect on concentration and learning. Some service providers noted the difficulty some young carers have in taking part in the out-of-school social activities in which many of their peers are involved.

A deputy headteacher spoke of the conflict that professionals feel when wishing to support the young person's caring role but also wanting to ensure that the young person's right to education is upheld:

Some of our condoned truancy, if I can put it that way, can be around caring. And it can be very difficult because you've got the needs of the domestic situation, which are very real, against the needs of this young person and their education. . . . What makes that very difficult is that sometimes you suspect that there's a mum here just not doing her bit and it's easy for the eldest daughter, or the son for that matter, but very often it's the daughter, to be looking after the little ones . . . you know . . . but it may be that mum actually does genuinely need help.

(deputy headteacher, mainstream school)

Professionals recognised the importance of strong partnerships between the school and the education welfare service, to ensure they make well-informed decisions about how best to address the non-attendance of a young carer. This might, for example, entail ensuring that a family or young person has access to particular forms of support. Alternatively, parents might be challenged about the extent to which they prioritise and support their child's education:

It's difficult when you're at arm's length . . . you know what the law says, you know what your responsibilities are, but you want to be a little bit human as well and you don't know frankly whether you are being conned again or what. And that's where the education welfare officers (EWOs) can be very helpful . . . make home visits and checking things out. We desperately need more [EWO] time.

(deputy headteacher)

Some service providers stressed how caring responsibilities can have a limiting effect on girls' aspirations, particularly when taking on the role of caring for younger siblings. One participant went so far as to suggest a link between caring, non-attendance and early pregnancy. He argued that for some girls, looking after younger siblings from an early age causes them to view themselves primarily as carers:

Many of these young people not attending school are carers . . . and then they stop being carers for other people and start being carers for their own children. Caring is one of the things they know they can do . . . and to care for their own child is the next rational step.

(co-ordinator of multi-agency support)

The detrimental effects of early caring responsibilities on girls' school performance is clearly an issue that warrants further attention. We maintain that school authorities have a responsibility to ensure that domestic situations do not override a young person's right to education. Where there are genuine caring needs additional support needs to be made available to the individual and her family.

Teenage pregnancy

Teenage birth rates in the UK are the highest in Western Europe. This phenomenon affects all parts of the country but is more pronounced in the poorest areas and among the most vulnerable, including those in public care and those who are excluded or disaffected from school (SEU, 1999). As we noted in chapter 2, the government sees teenage pregnancy as a problem, identifying it as both a cause and a consequence of social exclusion. The government's ten-year plan for reducing teenage pregnancy rates focuses on an awareness-raising campaign providing 'the facts about teenage pregnancy and parenthood' (SEU, 1999: 8); greater co-ordination between service providers; better prevention, including improved sex and relationship education; together with improved support for pregnant teenagers and young mothers to continue in education and to undertake training.

There remains widespread public and political concern about pregnant teenagers and schoolgirl mothers who tend to be represented in socially stigmatised ways. Within popular discourse, young single mothers are often presented as a drain on limited public resources. Their children are portrayed as contributing to the rise in youth crime. The government emphasises how high levels of teenage pregnancy serve to undermine efforts to achieve international economic competitiveness and a highly educated and skilled workforce, concluding that 'The UK cannot afford high rates of teenage conception and parenthood at the end of the 20th century' (SEU, 1999: 7). Implicit within government discourse is the need to reduce the number of young women dependent on state benefits, including housing support.

A small-scale study of pregnant teenagers and young mothers undertaken on a socially deprived Midlands city housing estate challenges the popular, stigmatised images of pregnant teenagers. Very few of the young women were living on their own and none had chosen early pregnancy as a way of accessing public sector housing.

Many received considerable support from their parents and grand-parents. While approximately half were on state benefits, most saw this as temporary and had plans to return to education or employ-ment (Rae, 2001).

We present professionals' and girls' perceptions of teenage preg-nancy and motherhood, examining these in the context of official policy relating to this particular group of girls and young women. We focus, in particular, on the specific educational challenges faced by those who experience pregnancy at a young age. A study carried out by the Audit Commission found that:

> One group that can easily lose out in their education is pregnant schoolgirls and schoolgirl mothers. In LEAs that could provide figures, there are usually more girls in this category than there are girls who are permanently excluded.
>
> (Audit Commission, 1999: 61)

Professionals in our study confirmed that young mothers and pregnant teenagers are a particularly vulnerable group whose edu-cational needs are poorly met. They present a complex relationship between pregnancy and exclusion, generally suggesting that girls whose low self-esteem, low aspirations or poor achievement had contributed to poor attendance are more likely to become pregnant than those who are well integrated into their schools. At the same time, although the regulations state that pregnancy should not be a reason for formal exclusion, pregnancy often leads to unofficial exclusion, school-condoned absence or self-exclusion. A co-ordinator of educational provision for pregnant teenagers noted that many of the pregnant teenagers in his area had not attended school recently. Many of them had not been formally excluded but had excluded themselves. The headteacher of a PRU that provides education for pregnant schoolgirls confirmed that: 'Many of the pregnant girls have self-excluded . . . or they haven't had positive experiences at school and their attendance has been poor'.

Professionals suggested that, for some girls, pregnancy is seen as a legitimate way of 'opting out' of education and as a means of feeling important, loved and grown up. Explanations concerning the rela-tively high rates of teenage pregnancy in the UK included peer group and media pressure on young women to be sexually active. Limited and/or poor-quality sex and relationship education was also cited as an explanation.

Pregnancy was seen by some as a form of self-exclusion. One service provider drew on the experiences of working with two pregnant girls to illustrate how a combination of factors had contributed to their pregnancy. She argued that pregnancy was seen as a 'legitimate way of opting out of school':

> To get pregnant, it's seen as a fairly outrageous thing to do . . . more so than telling someone to F off. It's a way of getting yourself notoriety. [With these two girls] it also gave them on the one hand something to love, which they needed, but also a legitimate way of opting out of school and I suppose exclusion would be a legitimate way of opting out of school for a lot a guys.
>
> (educational psychologist)

By contrast, an education welfare officer working with young people on a particular housing estate suggested that in that particular area pregnancy was viewed as a 'rite of passage'. She made reference to a popular soap opera where one of the teenage characters had recently had a baby. She explained that the girls with whom she worked saw this situation as quite normal but that they could not relate to the way in which the character in the television programme had been shunned by her friends and at school:

> And that's where the programme fell down for our girls here. It just would not happen like that here. A girl certainly wouldn't be excluded from her peer group. She would be a hero . . . they would all clutch round and look after her.
>
> (education welfare officer)

The same education welfare officer went on to suggest that for a minority of girls in this area pregnancy was actively sought as a way of feeling loved and cared for:

> We are aware of several socially insecure girls with real problem backgrounds who have been actively seeking pregnancy, because it is their access to grown-up life and access to the only time in their life when somebody fusses after them, takes care of them, and they are very important . . . and they have high status in the peer group.
>
> (education welfare officer)

Girls who took part in a group interview in that area confirmed that they all knew girls who were pregnant or who had a baby. The youngest they knew of was a 14-year-old. They suggested that such girls experience some stigmatisation but that they get emotional support from their friends:

> They get called all the names under the sun. Their friends will think it's pretty good though. They'll think: 'She can't be too irresponsible now 'cause she's got to look after herself plus a younger child'.
>
> (speaker in group interview)

The term 'younger child' suggests that the speaker still recognises a pregnant classmate as someone who has not yet attained adult status, despite the fact that she is pregnant and about to take on the responsibilities of becoming a parent. The need to be 'grown up' and responsible while at the same time lacking full adult status was also highlighted by two of the young mothers in Rae's (2001) study who commented:

> I'm not the baby anymore. I have to be the adult.
>
> I feel out of my depth. I'm still a kid too.
>
> (Rae, 2001: 29)

A service provider suggested that both low self-esteem and limited aspirations were contributory risk factors for some girls. She explained that in their work with young women they attempted to support girls in developing:

> Ambitions and aspirations which go beyond abusive relationships and reproducing at the first possible stage. We need to be able to show them that there is a way of feeling good about yourself without having it off with a succession of undesirable blokes.
>
> (head of PRU)

Service providers also argued that wider societal attitudes towards sex and gender relations played a part in explaining Britain's relatively high teenage pregnancy rates. Several participants emphasised that it is not simply lack of knowledge about contraception and safe sexual practices that contribute to high teenage pregnancy rates. Sex and relationship education needs to place more emphasis on communication and relationship issues and not just on the facts about sexual behaviour, reproduction and contraception:

> It's no use just doing work on sexual knowledge and contraception and reproduction. We need to do more on relationships between men and women.
>
> (co-ordinator of provision for pregnant schoolgirls)

This view was reiterated by another professional who spoke about her experiences working with a girls' group that was focusing on sexual health:

> And what we found was actually that the young people we were working with had a reasonable knowledge of contraception and safe sexual practices . . . but where they were falling down was that they were not assertive enough or confident enough. Their communication skills were not at a level where they could keep themselves safe.
>
> (children's rights officer)

Like most of the young mothers in Rae's (2001) study the young women with whom these professionals were working tended to have a good theoretical knowledge of contraception. Rae also observed that these young women were not confident in either saying 'no' or insisting on the use of contraception. For some of them sex was something which 'happened' to them. Those who could recall receiving any sex education reported that it had not been useful and had not included emotional aspects of sexual involvement or other relationship and communication issues. The professionals whom we interviewed considered it more important to focus on developing young women's communication skills, assertiveness and self-esteem than to provide information on safe sexual practices. These approaches contrast with the approach advocated in the Social Exclusion Unit's (1999) report on teenage pregnancy. Here the emphasis is more on the need for factual knowledge and less on the nature and quality of the relationships between men and women or the assertiveness and communication skills which young people may need. While ignorance about contraception and safe sexual practices is no doubt a contributory factor in some pregnancies, the service providers we interviewed suggested a reduction in teenage pregnancy rates will require addressing a much wider range of issues. As a review of research on teenage pregnancy concludes:

> Good sex education must incorporate the opportunity for young people to explore the personal, ethical and relationship issues surrounding sexual behaviour, in order that young women develop the skills and self-confidence to have greater control over their fertility.
>
> (Coleman and Dennison, 1998: 312)

Professionals in our study agreed with the government's assessment (SEU, 1999) that the low educational expectations and limited employment prospects of some girls contribute to relatively high teenage pregnancy rates. As one professional put it, 'Aspiration is the best form of contraceptive'. Noting this link between low educational attainment and teenage pregnancy, Coleman and Dennison (1998) argue for a holistic review of young women's needs:

> The more our society addresses the needs of young women, especially those who are not necessarily high achievers in the conventional sense, the less likely we are to see an increase in the rate of teenage pregnancy.
>
> (Coleman and Dennison, 1998: 312)

The approach they advocate contrasts with that in the Social Exclusion Unit's (1999) report *Teenage Pregnancy*, which fails to address some of these wider issues affecting girls. Official discourse, as presented in this report, locates the 'problem' of teenage pregnancy with a particularly vulnerable group of girls who are judged to have low aspirations and limited knowledge about contraception. The solution therefore lies in raising aspirations and providing factual knowledge. We suggest that the debate needs to be widened to encompass the needs of young women more generally and to address inequalities in gender relations. Given the links made within the SEU report between teenage pregnancy and disaffection from school, it is curious that the report neglects some of the issues raised by professionals and by girls in our study and discussed in previous chapters, namely the narrow definitions of success promoted in current policy discourse and the difficulties some girls experience with the curriculum, pedagogy, school organisation and ethos.

Sam, a Year 11 student, provided a lucid example of the links between teenage pregnancy and some of these wider issues. She spoke with considerable insight and compassion about the intersection of a range of factors that constituted a very effective barrier to the educational achievement of one of her classmates. Learning difficulties, low self-esteem, bullying and disaffection from school all played a part in her classmate's story. These difficulties were further compounded by pregnancy and the subsequent difficulties encountered in accessing education while coping with the care of a young child:

> There was this girl and she started to get bullied because she was very big built and they used to call her fatty and everything . . . but she wasn't. Then she started skipping days off school. They just thought she was skipping days off because she didn't like school. I think she missed 17 maybe 20 science lessons, then it was whole days, weeks and months. Then she left because she fell pregnant and then that was it. She's trying to get into college but she hasn't got any GCSEs and it'll be hard because she's got the baby. I really wanted her to have some more life. I wanted her to have an education . . . to just have something to help her but she never managed it. She's dyslexic as well but she's not statemented. She just thought to herself she was thick: 'I don't know nothing. I'm stupid', because people put her down and so she'd skip days off school.
>
> (Sam)

Despite widespread recognition of the value and cost-effectiveness of preventative work and early intervention, too often, educational support comes too little and too late. Sam's classmate's life chances might have been considerably improved if her learning needs and the issues of bullying and truanting had been more effectively addressed.

The service providers interviewed for this study raised a number of concerns relating to the specific educational needs of girls who were pregnant or who were young mothers. Few girls remained in school and for those educated in other settings provision was extremely limited, sometimes amounting to little more than three hours a week. Those who persisted with their education after giving birth encountered difficulties as the primary care-giver for a new baby. Referring to a Year 9 student, an education welfare officer explained:

If she keeps the baby it will be devastating [with regard to her future options]. She's bright, a good attender, but there has been some pressure from the boy and the boy's family for her to keep the baby. She will be referred to the pregnant schoolgirls' tuition service and can come back after the baby has been born but both her parents work. Realistically, this is the end of her formal education.

(education welfare officer)

The education welfare officer underlined her point by providing a further example of a student who had tried to return to school after having had a child:

It just wasn't possible . . . the poor girl was coming in, she was trying to do her best to be there and she'd been up all night with a baby who was teething.

This is the meaning of exclusion, isn't it? So if a girl made that dreadful mistake and became pregnant at an early age, she is excluded. There is no way she can take part . . . and there is still the stigma and accusation: 'Why should the government bother about *them?*'

(education welfare officer)

Young mothers faced difficulties, first, in accessing any education and second, in combining their education with new childcare responsibilities. The barriers make it very difficult to gain qualifications, engage in further training or education and achieve longer-term employment. Lack of affordable childcare was considered to be the major barrier preventing young mothers from returning to education. A number of service providers argued that practical measures such as having a school-based crèche would make it easier for young mothers to return:

It's an institutional barrier. You can't say 'come back to school but by the way don't bring your child with you, we've got no provision'.

(co-ordinator of multi-agency support)

Have a crèche attached to a school . . . if you really want to encourage pupil parents to stay in the system.

(educational welfare officer)

Low expectations

Interviews with service providers highlighted concerns about the low expectations of many working-class girls which may serve as a barrier to educational success. The problem is complex: as we have seen in chapter 4, our own interviews with girls revealed some tensions between a widespread desire to achieve academic success, limited knowledge about the range of post-16 educational and training opportunities, and career choices which tended towards traditionally feminine (and often low-paid) occupations. The vast majority of the students we interviewed were from working-class backgrounds and the student population of all but one of the mainstream schools they attended was more or less exclusively working-class. A minority of our student sample had aspirations to attend university and seek professional employment. Notably, interviewees from black and South Asian communities tended to have higher aspirations. These girls spoke of the encouragement and support they received from their parents, and some that had encountered considerable difficulties earlier in their school careers were working to overcome these.

Yet service providers from each of the areas in which we carried out our research spoke at length of the low aspirations of some girls and their parents, suggesting that in comparison with boys, girls do not have many ideas about what they want to do after they leave school. In particular, girls were often judged to have low levels of self-esteem and personal confidence. Social class, poverty and the low educational attainment of parents were seen as impacting on the aspirations of these girls.

> Parents have such negative recollections of school themselves, and were themselves low achievers and find it very difficult to promote higher education among their children.
>
> (head of behaviour support service)

> They don't see futures for themselves apart from tomorrow. Nobody's ever said, 'this is what you can do' . . . and it's harder to get jobs now.
>
> (head of service for children in public care)

> And there's something about self-esteem and confidence as well . . . a lack of self-confidence. I think it happens to boys as well, but not to the same degree.
>
> (children's rights officer)

Some service providers argued that girls need particular support in developing assertive and confident relationships with parents and with fellow students, particularly boys:

> Confidence . . . to be assertive in their relationships, to be able to ask for what they need and want to know, not feeling like they have to comply with other people's wishes.
>
> (youth worker)

> Aspirations are central to all this. Encouraging girls to be more assertive is important . . . and to see beyond being carers. Caring is important but there are other things as well.
>
> (co-ordinator of multi-agency support)

A number of interviewees suggested that there is still a dominant belief among some parents that educational achievement is more important for boys than for girls, since boys are expected to be the prime income earners, and girls the prime caregivers. One professional working in a school with a working-class population observed:

> There are a small number of high-achieving families where parents will support their daughters as well as their sons and will want them to go on to sixth form college to do A levels and to further education . . . but it's a small percentage.
>
> (education welfare officer)

Another service provider noted how some of the most disadvantaged girls viewed education as a way of changing their lives for the better:

> There are some girls that really push and want to work and get out of the traps that are there for them. Some of them see getting an education as a way of leaving the sort of life they have behind . . . but not the majority.
>
> (head of service for children in public care)

Recent research has suggested that mother–daughter relationships within 'transitional' working-class families, where values are in the process of changing, have been found to support girls' school achievement by emphasising the importance of independence, and providing emotional support through talking and listening and influencing girls' values (Mann, 1998). Certainly, a number of girls within our sample who had overcome difficult behaviour patterns and negative teacher expectations had gained this kind of support from their mothers.

Some service providers expressed concern about the expectations of girls from South Asian communities. While some suggested that parents within these communities had somewhat limited horizons for their daughters, others were concerned that fellow professionals continued to expect little from these girls, believing them to be confined by family expectations. A number reflected on the ways in which a particular girls' school was raising achievement levels and aspirations, but others felt that a number of South Asian girls continue to encounter tensions:

> Some girls still might find themselves in conflict between the expectations of their families and the school ... what they could achieve if they wanted to go on further in education.
>
> (head of behaviour support service)

Others acknowledged the diversity within the grouping they defined as 'Asian'. One service provider illustrated how her experience in organising sporting opportunities had highlighted the need to ensure that appropriate steps are taken to accommodate different needs and traditions within what might appear to an outsider to be a homogeneous group:

> The fact that they were Asian girls didn't unite them. There were vast differences ... different religions and even within the same religion there were still lots of differences depending on parental and family values. For people not working with those cultures and religions, it's easy to lump them all together and make assumptions and stereotypes.
>
> (children's rights officer)

There is growing evidence of more open attitudes within various South Asian communities towards the education of girls (for example, Basit, 1997; Parker-Jenkins et al., 1999) which challenges some of the stereotypes held by some professionals working with these young people. These and other researchers highlight how cultural, religious and personal identities are fluid and are constantly being negotiated and re-negotiated.

Service providers argued that all girls, and especially working-class girls from diverse backgrounds, needed professional support in broadening their views of life choices and possibilities:

> They aren't really encouraged to explore other possibilities. We need to make sure they know there are other options . . . other than having a baby as soon as you finish school. And if you are a young parent, there are still educational opportunities.
>
> (youth worker)

Sexual vulnerability

Some professionals identified peer pressure on girls to be sexually active as a potential barrier to educational achievement. They suggested that some girls seek to project an image of themselves as desirable and sexually experienced as a way of gaining peer status. Others spoke of how relationships with older boys sometimes led to lateness or non-attendance at school. A small number highlighted sexual exploitation as a serious but hidden problem affecting the education of some girls:

> There's a real demand for 13, 14, 15 year olds . . . and I know a lot of women who have got caught up in this through escort agencies . . . and that can have a serious effect on their education.
>
> (children's rights officer)

A key concern was the lack of services for those at risk of sexual exploitation. This is linked to wider social attitudes that make it difficult to acknowledge and address the problem:

> I think that's a real cultural problem in this country whereby we have this acceptance that men can and do pay for sex with young women. It's like it's brushed under the carpet and ignored.
>
> (children's rights officer)

For sexually vulnerable girls, drugs were sometimes both a means of drawing them into prostitution and a way of coping with that involvement:

Drug use is an issue for both sexes, but for the girls that are
sexually vulnerable, it's even more of an issue because it's part
of the way I think they are encouraged to become involved in it
[sexual exploitation]. They are needy and can be manipulated
and I think they do it to forget what is going on 'cause otherwise
life is unbearable.

(head of PRU)

Drug and alcohol use

Drug and alcohol use, however, was clearly perceived as a growing
problem. The headteacher in one PRU reported responding to this
by building a drug education package into the students' induction
programme and providing staff with training. A number of service
providers drew attention to the use of drugs such as cannabis and
speed, arguing that drug use served as a barrier to educational
achievement. For professionals working with young people on a
particular housing estate, the impact of heroin use and associated
crime was thought to have an impact on the whole community,
undermining children's security and well-being:

Drugs are an issue. Heroin is very big in this area and it affects
them. Even if they are not using themselves, it's very much in
their lives with family members using, dealing or being involved
in criminal activities to support their habit. It is easy for them to
get into it . . . just where they are . . . where they're growing up.

(youth worker)

In a climate of competition between schools, student involvement
with drugs is a sensitive issue and one which some professionals felt
was being kept hidden. Participants suggested that teachers sometimes suspect drug use or drug dealing, but in the absence of firm
proof schools are unwilling to investigate, preferring to overlook the
impact of drugs on behaviour. For example, they suggested that
some instances of violence, theft and non-attendance may be drug-
related but schools do not necessarily record or address this in their
disciplinary procedures. Reluctance to acknowledge the impact of
drug use means that few steps are taken to tackle this growing
problem.

The challenge of inclusion

Service providers examined some of the initiatives being taken to develop more inclusive learning environments for girls. We focus on two broad approaches: the development of special facilities for girls within mainstream schools and the use of under-16 placements at further education colleges. These initiatives are set in the context of professionals' reflections on girls' friendships and support networks and how these can both enable and undermine efforts to promote inclusion.

Some service providers argued that the importance to girls of being part of a friendship group meant that a breakdown in friend-ships had potentially more impact on their learning and well-being compared to boys. Others recognised the impact of personal rela-tionship difficulties on girls' lives but not necessarily on their learning:

> Probably the business of girls falling out . . . of being friends and then not being friends . . . certainly Year 9, Year 10 can be an absolute nightmare for some groups of girls, but it isn't so directly confrontational with the learning culture. It's very much a personal domestic if you like . . . but it's not as estab-lished as 'really cool boys don't achieve'. There's not that direct impinging on learning within the school.
>
> (deputy headteacher)

Teachers may only partially recognise the detrimental effects of friendship break-ups or verbal or psychological bullying on girls' concentration and learning (Crozier and Anstiss, 1995; Hey, 1997; Stanley and Arora, 1998). As we have shown in chapter 4, girls in this study were quick to identify the negative impact of bullying and relationship problems on their own learning and on the learning of others. As their evidence confirms, the less visible forms of psycho-logical bullying used by girls (name-calling, the starting of rumours, social exclusion) mean that both the extent of the problem and its impact are often underestimated, causing school authorities not to respond with the same urgency as to physical forms of bullying.

Girls only groups

As we have discussed in chapter 5, a number of girls in this study felt it would be helpful if 'girls only' spaces were created in school.

A number of service providers had been involved in establishing girls' groups as part of their work. Some of these were short-term initiatives to meet specific needs such as a school-based 'self-esteem' group and a group addressing 'health' in another local authority. Others were established as part of the ongoing programmes on offer and some were at a pilot stage. The accounts given highlight some of the concerns that lead to the development of such groups and underline the value and importance of creating some 'girls only' spaces.

A youth worker noted that it was generally much easier to attract young men to a group than young women. He spoke of social isolation, low confidence and low self-esteem as barriers preventing some young people from accessing services, suggesting that girls are likely to encounter such barriers, particularly in relation to youth clubs:

> We see that as one of the problems of a youth club. It is often people that feel happy in a big social group [that come]. The only thing is that some of the young women . . . particularly those lacking in self-esteem . . . won't come to a youth club at all. They are not confident enough about themselves.
>
> (youth worker)

A worker in another area confirmed this and spoke of a growing awareness among her colleagues that girls were 'out there' on the estate but were not coming in and using the centre. Consultation with girls suggested that programmes needed to be modified to meet their specific interests and needs. She suggested that many youth clubs are seen to be male dominated and that consequently many girls do not even want to come in. She argued that in a mixed gender setting girls will get a 'hard time' from the boys for not being good at activities like snooker and sport, so further discouraging them from using the centre.

One LEA behaviour support service had piloted a programme for girls. Staff were concerned about the way in which girls' needs tended to be overlooked in mixed schools, with few being referred to their service. Teachers in girls' schools who were seeking support for their students had also approached them:

> I could see examples of girls where we knew there was something wrong, but they weren't tackled because they didn't

behave like the boys did. I could go into some mixed schools, and would have sixteen kids on my caseload and none of them girls. These are schools in special measures, where behaviour is an issue, where there is social deprivation, and yet the girls aren't referred . . . and I couldn't believe it really. Their needs just weren't addressed.

(head of behavioural support centre)

In another example, a girls' group was again established as a way of attracting referrals of girls from a range of agencies who were previously only considering boys. The belief underlying the development of this group was that catering for girls' interests and needs sometimes meant doing things without their male peers. The key worker also identified the teasing and harassment of girls that can occur in male-dominated mixed-gender settings. She noted the slow process of getting agencies to recognise the needs of girls who tend to present their problems in different ways from boys:

The message was slowly getting through to people . . . not as much as I would like but maybe a little bit in terms of needs [for girls]. 'Cause you know, when I started, it was like, young male, been permanently excluded or at risk of exclusion . . . and everybody was looking at it that way. So we've tried to broaden it out.

(manager of project for disaffected young people)

Each of these initiatives was based on a broader concept of exclusion than is often adopted among professionals working with young people.

Further Education (FE) colleges

Service providers generally viewed special placements at FE colleges for some under-16 year olds in a positive light. However, some reservations were expressed. First, it was argued that some students lacked the maturity and skills for independent learning. Second, it was argued that college placements sometimes constituted 'exclusion by the back door'. Finally, it was suggested that placements offered girls rather limited options, which often reinforced sex-stereotyped vocational options.

Some referrals to FE colleges were thought inappropriate for individuals who lacked the skills to successfully manage the college environment. This could lead to further failure and disengagement:

> I'm a bit loath to get Year 9 and 10s into college because they just cannot cope. Social workers and some schools are too ready to say: 'OK, we'll get you a college placement'. It's very difficult for them to survive in college. They can't build up the [peer] relationships in colleges that they can in schools because they all go to various places . . . and the failure rate . . . or the self-exclusion from college is much greater than from school. It's a different way of being educated. Basically, the responsibility is on themselves to get them there . . . and some of them just don't cope with that.
>
> (head of service for children in public care)

While some might challenge these assertions about failure and self-exclusion rates (indeed, our own investigations found encouraging results with regard to attendance and achievement), the argument that there are some pupils for whom an FE placement will not be appropriate is valid and important.

Some college placements may effectively be informal and unrecorded permanent exclusions from school. As the head of a PRU explained, requirements to reduce exclusion rates meant that more and more of the students referred to her centre had not been formally excluded but had come into the centre for a period of time as part of a pastoral support programme. The aim is to return them to school or to an alternative such as a college course. She suspected that in some cases, the main motive of the school was to remove the student without serious consideration of their re-integration. In such cases parents have little say in what happens to their child:

> The school says they don't want them back in school but they've got to do something with them, so they put them on a fixed-term exclusion. They will come here for a few weeks while a college placement is organised and the family will be told later that this is the plan.
>
> (head of PRU)

This interviewee suggested a college placement is also financially attractive to the school. Although the school will have to transfer money to the college to cover the placement, the costs are generally less than the loss of income if the student is permanently excluded and removed from the school's roll. It is important that whatever processes are in place, that they are transparent, allowing both students and parents to participate fully in decision-making.

Most girls accessing college placements are making very limited subject choices, based on a narrow range of traditionally female vocational options, such as hairdressing, beauty therapy and childcare:

> A few will go on and do more academic courses . . . but even those will tend to do the relatively clear female things. We try very hard here. We get girls doing science and technology. We have boys doing childcare courses . . . but still at the end of it, something sends them off in those [stereotyped] directions.
>
> (head of PRU)

The developing policy of placing under-16 year olds in FE colleges is designed to ensure their educational inclusion. If, by accessing traditionally feminine vocational options the majority of girls are channelled into low-paid work, then the overall aim of longer-term social inclusion may be seriously compromised.

Service providers identified considerable barriers to girls' educational inclusion. They also identified a number of strategies for overcoming such barriers. Success in breaking down barriers will require professionals to work more closely with girls and their families and to listen to girls' perspectives. It will also require professionals to challenge their own stereotypes and for policy-makers to address some of the hidden features of a society which maintains unequal gender relations, leaving many girls vulnerable to various forms of sexual exploitation.

Part III

Including girls

Chapter 7

Lessons for schools
and policy-makers

Our study reveals a complex picture of the ways in which girls can be excluded from school. Although girls are less likely to experience permanent disciplinary exclusion than their male peers, they remain subject to other forms of exclusion, including informal and self-exclusion. These types of exclusion leave girls particularly vulnerable to longer-term social exclusion as they often fail to trigger the support that individuals need. Given that young women remain disadvantaged in the labour market, this is a particularly blatant injustice.

The efforts of policy-makers to address the needs of boys, examining apparent 'underachievement' and disaffection, have led to a neglect of girls' social and educational needs. At school level, the more overtly challenging behaviour of some boys has served to mask girls' difficulties, resulting in programmes, provision and resource allocation targeted at boys. We have uncovered what has been a relatively hidden problem of exclusion among girls.

We have demonstrated how many of the difficulties experienced by girls in school are also of a hidden nature. Whether the issue is one of learning difficulties, caring responsibilities, bullying or relationship problems, girls' problems and needs may not always be obvious to the professionals who work with them. This may be because an individual's response or way of dealing with the issue is not one that immediately attracts the attention of adults or because adults do not recognise the concern as significant. One coping strategy is to seek to resolve problems without adult support. A number of girls expressed a preference for resolving problems in this way.

The girls made a direct link between bullying (including psychological and verbal bullying) and exclusion. This link was not generally recognised by the professionals in our study. Girls tend to attach tremendous importance to friendship and social networks. Yet a number of teachers and other professionals either fail to recognise, or under-estimate, the potentially damaging impact that a rift between friends or isolation within a class can have on an individual's welfare and academic attainment.

Girls experience difficulties in accessing appropriate support. Their needs are varied and often complex, yet services tend to be compartmentalised. Access is usually dependent on professional referral. Although there has been investment in support systems and alternative educational provision for young people in difficulties, many programmes which are formally open to both sexes have in fact been designed to meet the specific interests and needs of boys. Parents may not be in a position to offer their daughter appropriate or sustained support and, indeed, are not always aware of school-based problems. This, again, is a feature of girls' often internalised and less disruptive responses to unhappiness.

Self-exclusion from school is a strategy often reluctantly adopted by girls and young women who have failed to find appropriate support. Most of the girls in our study attached great importance to education and those who had previously absented themselves from school regretted their actions.

Educational provision for young women who are pregnant and for young mothers is inadequate. While official policy confirms that pregnancy is not a reason for exclusion from school, in practice pregnancy and motherhood often mark the end of a girl's formal education. Those who have had successful school careers and who are well motivated are equally likely to encounter barriers to their continuing education as those who have previous experiences of exclusion. In particular, childcare facilities in schools and colleges are likely to be extremely limited.

Official discourse continues to present teenage motherhood as a problem, and girls who become pregnant are likely to experience public criticism and stigmatisation. The culture of blame attached to young mothers is matched by official policies which tend to explain early pregnancy in terms of ignorance about contraception and safe sexual practices. Relatively little official attention has been given to the need for programmes which address relationships between the sexes or which promote self-esteem, confidence and choice. Many young mothers have a history of difficulties at school and complex needs requiring a range of support services, but the compartmentalisation of services makes access problematic.

Ironically, although young mothers are often presented in the media as 'welfare scroungers' or 'queue-jumpers', the minority who manage to pursue their education are more likely to be supported by their families than by the state. These families (often the student's mother or grandmother) offer childcare and other support, since publicly funded facilities are not generally available.

Girls are generally not a priority in schools' thinking about behaviour management and school exclusion. Even when girls' problems are recognised, professionals may be reluctant to refer girls to alternative schemes and programmes, judging such provision to be inappropriate and/or male dominated. Many of the girls we interviewed felt that schools use exclusion and other disciplinary sanctions inconsistently, with clear differences between what teachers class as acceptable behaviour from boys and girls. Others highlighted differences in teacher expectations and treatment of different groupings of girls, influenced by such factors as ethnicity and 'reputation'. Professionals also reported differences in the ways in which boys and girls are disciplined.

School effectiveness debates have been given high priority on the international educational policy agenda. The focus is on raising achievement, as defined in terms of improved public examination results. Schools are often faced with an apparent dilemma in seeking to be inclusive of 'difficult' young people or those in difficulties, since school effectiveness has been largely defined by a narrow range of academic indicators. We argue that the range of school effectiveness indicators needs to be broadened to encompass the extent to which institutions are able to support and include young people in difficulties.

In England, the publication of league tables has put additional pressure on schools to focus on academic goals. As we discussed in chapter 2, other equally important educational outcomes have subsequently been accorded less attention. The 'effectiveness' of any given secondary school is judged, to a very high degree, by the percentage of students that achieve GCSE grades A–C. We do not wish to suggest that academic goals are not important. Indeed, we acknowledge (as did the vast majority of young women in our study) that academic success at school opens up a wide range of choices, particularly for young people in disadvantaged circumstances. Our concern, which is supported by the evidence of both the students and the professionals whom we interviewed, is that many young women are failing to realise their academic potential at school because other educational and social needs are going unaddressed. Others are placed under extreme pressure to perform, but lack appropriate support. These young women are then vulnerable to various forms of school exclusion. Policies designed to promote school effectiveness have an unintended exclusionary outcome.

We argue that if schools address the needs of those girls who are currently excluded, they are also likely to improve their overall examination performance. Given the link between poor attendance and poor achievement, policies aimed at reducing disaffection and promoting achievement will also need to address some of the specific causes of non-attendance among girls. A more inclusive school culture does not imply a less effective school. On the contrary, a school which is more inclusive of girls is likely to prove a more effective school, even if a very narrow set of academic indicators is used to measure effectiveness.

Any examination of the ways in which girls are included or excluded from school also needs to consider their situation beyond school and, in particular, their access to further education and training. Some service providers expressed concern that family expectations and teachers' assumptions about family expectations were likely to influence schools' expectations of particular students. They argued that some colleagues assumed that girls from minority ethnic communities and those living in particularly disadvantaged areas were unlikely to pursue a full range of post-16 options and choices. They were concerned that these professional assumptions have an impact on young people's attainment and on the information they receive about their options beyond school. Our study revealed that although girls in alternative educational provision, such as PRUs, were usually well informed about further education and training opportunities, this was generally not the case for those in mainstream education.

One belief underpinning this study is that young people have an important contribution to make to debates about policy and practice in education. Their experiences place them in a unique position to make assessments about the quality and effectiveness of schooling systems and to make recommendations on how these might be improved. By developing a research project which placed particular emphasis on girls' understandings of schooling, our intention is to broaden the debates about effective schools. We have sought to demonstrate that teachers, schools and policy-makers can learn a great deal from girls' experiences and to highlight how learners can make a positive contribution to the realisation of more effective schools. We therefore reflect on the practice and policy implications of our research for schools, alternative education providers and government. We are particularly conscious of the need for early intervention strategies that seek to prevent the exclusion of girls and young women from school and which will thus support schools in becoming inclusive communities.

What schools can do

We suggest that schools need to review their pastoral support systems to identify the ways in which they meet the specific needs of girls. Clear plans are needed for the integration of all categories of student who have been out of school, including those absent as a result of formal exclusion, truancy, long-term illness and pregnancy. Since girls are subject to a variety of forms of exclusion from school (disciplinary processes, withdrawal, truancy and self-exclusion), the ways in which these processes may interact in particular cases needs to be understood. For example, in developing plans for the re-integration of a student who has a history of truanting, the underlying causes of her truancy need to be understood. Thus a re-integration plan which fails to take into consideration learning difficulties, for example, may result in frustration and lead to behaviour which results in disciplinary exclusion.

Our research has identified the need for support which can be accessed on a self-referral basis, such as a school counsellor or school nurse. Students need to be confident that their privacy is safeguarded, that their consent will be sought in any subsequent interventions and that they are consulted in any decision-making processes. Such interventions and support for individuals identified as vulnerable need to be discreet and sensitive as girls and young women are often concerned about peer reactions and reputation. Specific initiatives to support girls need to recognise differences in needs between girls, related, for example, to ethnicity, sexuality, maturity and out-of-school responsibilities. Access to support systems, alternative curricular arrangements and other opportunities should be monitored by ethnicity and gender, as should the application of any exclusionary sanctions.

Policies and practices that address bullying need to acknowledge verbal and psychological bullying to which girls may be particularly vulnerable, as well as physical aggression. Schools need to address

racial harassment as a particular form of bullying. Policies and practices need to be implemented alongside education programmes for
students and training and support for staff.

We have noted how effective student consultation and participation structures and procedures are critical in the development of
inclusive schools. These may include student councils, involvement
in drawing up codes of conduct and consultation on policy development. In setting up such procedures schools need to be sensitive
to the differing needs of boys and girls and to recognise diversity
within these broad groupings. Our research confirms that girls, and
by extension, all students, can support schools in becoming more
inclusive communities, working effectively to meet the varied needs
of their members. More democratic schools are likely to be more
inclusive and better disciplined institutions.

What providers of alternative education can do

With the exception of specific schemes to meet the needs of pregnant school-age girls and young mothers, providers tend to offer
programmes which, although in principle are open to both boys and
girls, tend to cater for the needs of boys. There appears to be very
little monitoring of students referred to alternative educational provision, either by gender or ethnicity. This appears to be the case
whether the provision is publicly funded (for example, FE college
places for under-16 year-olds), or where voluntary organisations are
the providers. Our research suggests that improved communication
and clear contracts between alternative providers and schools would
help support the successful re-integration of students participating
in short-term alternative programmes.

We recommend that providers of alternative education monitor
both the uptake and the outcomes of their programmes by gender
and ethnicity and that they consider offering some programmes
exclusively for girls. Consultation processes which include young
women may enable the better targeting of programmes. There is a
need to liaise more effectively with schools and local authorities.

What local authorities and government departments can do

Local education authorities can play a leading role in helping put girls' needs back on the agenda. They also have a potentially influential role in enabling greater co-operation between various professional groups working with young women and in enabling more effective inter-agency working. For example, our research suggests that the development of multi-disciplinary teams attached to schools may be a useful step in meeting the needs of vulnerable young people. Local authorities and government departments can play a key role in helping schools to monitor and interpret their exclusion and truancy statistics. The importance of this monitoring and feedback role is increasingly recognised. As an official document from New Zealand notes:

> [W]e are giving schools much more information about their stand-down and suspension numbers and how they compare with other schools. This information helps principals and boards to recognise when they need to take action.
>
> (Ministry of Education, 2001: 3).

Such information can usefully include commentaries on exclusion statistics, monitored by ethnicity and gender, which highlight girls' needs even when they form a small proportion of those formally excluded. Schools can be provided with comparisons with other schools in similar circumstances and examples of best practice from other institutions.

We have seen how an emphasis by both government and the media on boys' achievement and boys' disaffection has led to a neglect among some professionals of girls' needs. Government departments need to redress the balance, recognising the link between exclusion from school and women's levels of education which have an impact both on families and employment prospects. Girls' exclusion from school is a human rights issue, but it is also one with considerable social and economic implications. No government can afford to neglect significant numbers of young women or leave them to long-term social exclusion.

The evidence from the girls in this study provides vivid illustrations of how schools can become more inclusive of girls, enabling them to feel a genuine sense of belonging and achievement. It also demonstrates how more inclusive schools might also become more effective schools. If we are to address social exclusion, it will be necessary to focus on school exclusion *in all its forms* rather than on the less frequent but more easily measured practice of formal permanent exclusion.

Our contribution to the 'gender jigsaw' (Collins *et al.*, 2000a) has been to look beyond the achievement data in order to understand girls' experiences of school, particularly their experiences of inclusion and exclusion. We have presented the arguments for keeping girls as well as boys at the centre of the educational policy agenda, in order to achieve genuine social and educational inclusion. The challenge remains to tackle the contradictions within education systems between inclusionary policies and intentions on the one hand and exclusionary practices on the other.

Notes

Introduction

1 Further details of the six sample areas are provided in our research report *Not a Problem? Girls and school exclusion* (Osler et al., 2002). The three contrasting LEAs were an urban area in the north of England, a large metropolitan LEA in the Midlands and a unitary authority in the South. The three education action zones were situated in the South East, the Midlands and an inner London borough. The sample was designed to encompass both urban and rural areas and areas of high and low economic deprivation.

2 'n'-numbers refer to the number of participants in the sample.

Chapter I

1 A student's point score is calculated by awarding 10 points at A level for the top grade A, 8 points for B, 6 for C, 4 for D and 2 for E. AS grades are awarded half the number of points, with a grade A scoring 5 points, grade B 4 points, and so on.

Chapter 2

1 In May 2002 a judge reminded school governing bodies that their discipline committees were statutory and that such a committee 'most certainly was not there to rubber stamp the headteachers' decision'. Unless the committee acted as an independent reviewing body, 'it served no purpose whatsoever'. Although he dismissed an application for a judicial review, following the decision of a committee of governors and that of an independent appeal panel to uphold the decision of the headteacher to permanently exclude a boy from Kingsmead secondary school, Enfield, he left the door open for future reviews, noting that the fact that an appeal had been heard by an independent panel did not prevent a parent from going to the courts over a discipline committee decision (Johnson, 2002: 31).

2 The term 'stand-down' is used in New Zealand to apply to a fixed-term exclusion lasting up to five days.

3 We are not arguing that young people do not also have obligations, since human rights are only guaranteed when the principle of reciprocity is enacted (Osler and Starkey, 2000b and 2001a).
4 Young people are judged to be less likely than their elders to engage in political activities and are less likely to exercise their right to vote. This viewpoint has been challenged by research (Roker *et al.*, 1999). For a discussion of this deficit model of young people and particularly young people from ethnic minority communities which has informed the development of the citizenship curriculum see Osler, 2000, and Osler and Starkey, 2001b, 2002b.

Chapter 3

1 From January 2002 the Department for Education and Skills is collecting Pupil Level Annual School Census (PLASC) data which will permit an analysis by ethnicity and gender of school exclusions and of student attainment. A wide range of information is available from PLASC including type of exclusion (e.g. fixed-term or permanent), SEN provision, free school meals and postcode data. In 2001–02 we developed, on behalf of the DfES, a searchable database which captures key information from LEA action plans for spending the Ethnic Minority Achievement Grant. LEAs submitted data on the attainment of pupils from different ethnic groupings. Unfortunately, they were not required to provide in their action plans information on attainment by ethnicity *and* gender.
2 For example, *On Track* and *Crime Reduction in Secondary Schools* are Home Office initiatives that support the education of vulnerable young people. The Department of Health supports several school-based projects aimed at identifying and addressing mental health problems in schools, through the CAMHS Innovation Mental Health Grant.
3 An example of an initiative requiring a multi-agency approach is the *Connexions* service, which provides mentoring, career guidance and personal support for young people in the transition from school to further education and training. Central government has sought to model an inter-agency approach through inter-ministerial initiatives such as that developed jointly by the Department of Health and the Department for Education and Employment to tackle the underachievement of children in public care (DfEE, 2000).
4 This in-school centre, funded through the Excellence in Cities programme, was a new initiative providing support for students with behaviour difficulties. Once allocated to the centre, each student was allocated a mentor who worked with them on learning and behavioural goals, before assisting their re-integration into their mainstream classes. At the time of our visit the centre was supporting ten boys and two girls. No African Caribbean students had been referred. The head of the centre voiced a concern that African Caribbean students might be being excluded before they were able to access an appropriate support service.
5 Just ten out of the 20 FE colleges we surveyed that provided courses for under-16s were able to provide a gender breakdown for the students that

accessed these programmes. The percentage of girls participating in the programmes ranged from 0 to 48. One college noted that the increasing percentage of girls (40 per cent at the time of our enquiry) was due to active encouragement in schools about the importance of ensuring that they consider the needs of both boys and girls. In the words of this interviewee, 'There is probably the same number of disaffected girls as boys in schools, but it is the boys that tend to get picked up'.

6 See chapter 1 for a discussion and critique of these discourses.

7 Other researchers have noted the low prevalence of behavioural problems such as Conduct Disorder (CD), Attention Deficit Hyperactivity Disorder (ADHD) and Oppositional Defiant Disorder (ODD) among girls and attribute this, in part, to gender biases in diagnostic criteria. For example, physical aggression is one of the criteria for CD. However, 'indirect' or 'social aggression' is much more likely to be used among girls (Keenan *et al.*, 1999).

8 The influence of girls' aspirations and the gendered nature of subject choices and how these impact on access to alternative placements is discussed in chapters 4 and 6.

Chapter 4

1 Setting, or so-called 'ability grouping', is a common practice. Students in lower sets are often entered for tiered GCSE examination papers where the best achievable grade is a C or lower. Such students then find that their access to future education and training is limited. See Gillborn and Youdell (2000) for a discussion of tiered exams and chapter 5 for students' views of setting.

2 In exploring the concept of 'academic exclusion', Benjamin (2000) argues that some school practices, including the language of 'special needs', construct what academically excluded students experience as a second-class version of success.

References

Adonis, A. (2001) 'High challenge, high support', *Policy Network*, 1: 5–15.

Ahmad, F. (2001) 'Modern traditions? British women and academic achievement', *Gender and Education*, 13 (2): 137–52.

Ainscow, M., Farrell, P., Tweddle, D. and Malki, G. (1999) 'The role of LEAs in developing inclusive policies and practices', *British Journal of Special Education*, 26 (3): 136–40.

Alibhai-Brown, Y. (2001) *Who Do We Think We Are? Imagining the New Britain*, London: Penguin.

Alton-Lee, A. and Praat, A. (2001) *Questioning Gender: snapshots from explaining and addressing gender differences in the New Zealand compulsory school sector*, Wellington: Ministry of Education, Research and Evaluation (Internal) Unit.

Arnot, M., David, M. and Weiner, G. (1996) *Educational Reforms and Gender Equality in Schools*, Manchester: Equal Opportunities Commission.

—— (1999) *Closing the Gender Gap: post-war education and social change*, Cambridge: Polity Press.

Audit Commission (1996) *Misspent Youth: young people and crime*, London: Audit Commission.

—— (1999) *Missing Out: LEA management of school attendance and exclusion*, London: Audit Commission.

Ballard, K. (1999) 'International voices: an introduction', in K. Ballard (ed.) *Inclusive Education: international voices on disability and justice*, pp. 1–9, London: Falmer Press.

Basit, T. (1997) 'I want more freedom, but not too much: British Muslim girls and the dynamism of family values', *Gender and Education*, 9 (4): 425–39.

Benjamin, S. (2000) 'Differently successful? Academic in/exclusion in a girls' comprehensive school', paper presented at the International Special Education Congress, University of Manchester, July.

Biddulph, S. (1997) *Raising Boys*, Lane Cove, Australia: Finch Publishing.

Blair, M. (2001) *Why Pick On Me? School exclusion and black youth*, Stoke: Trentham.

Bloch, M. and Vavrus, F. (1998) 'Gender and educational research, policy, and practice in sub-Saharan Africa: theoretical and empirical problems and prospects', in M. Bloch, J. A. Beoku-Betts and B. R. Tabachnick (eds) *Women and Education in Sub-Saharan Africa: power, opportunities and constraints*, pp. 1–24, Boulder, Colorado: Lynne Rienner.

Boaler, J., Wiliam, D. and Brown, M. (2000) 'Students' experiences of ability grouping – disaffection, polarisation and the construction of failure', *British Educational Research Journal*, 26 (5): 631–48.

Bourne, J., Bridges, L. and Searle, C. (eds) (1994) *Outcast England: how schools exclude black children*, London: Institute for Race Relations.

Brooks, M., Milne, C., Paterson, K., Johannson, K. and Hart, K. (1997) *Under-age School Leaving: a report to the National Youth Affairs Research Scheme*, Hobart: National Clearing House of Youth Studies.

Bullen, E. Kenway, J. and Hey, V. (2000) 'New Labour, social exclusion and educational risk management: the case of 'gymslip mums'', *British Educational Research Journal*, 26 (4): 441–56.

Carter, C. and Osler, A. (2000) 'Human rights, identities and conflict management: a study of school culture as experienced through classroom relationships', *Cambridge Journal of Education*, 30 (3): 335–56.

Chebel d'Appollonia, A. (1998) *Les Racismes Ordinaires*, Paris: Presses de Sciences Politiques.

Coard, B. (1971) *How the West Indian Child is made Educationally Subnormal in the British School System*, London: New Beacon Books.

Coleman, J. and Dennison, C. (1998) 'Teenage parenthood, research review', *Children and Society*, 12: 306–14.

Collins, C., Kenway, J. and McLeod, J. (2000a) 'Gender debates we still have to have', *Australian Educational Researcher*, 27 (3): 37–48.

—— (2000b) *Factors Influencing Educational Performance of Males and Females in School and their Initial Destinations after Leaving School*, Department of Education, Training and Youth Affairs, Canberra. http://www.detya.gov.au/schools/publications/index.htm

Commission for Racial Equality (1988) *Ethnic Minority School Teachers: a survey in eight local education authorities*, London: CRE.

—— (1997) *Exclusion from School and Racial Equality: good practice guide*, London: CRE.

Connolly, P. (1998) *Racism, Gender Identities and Young Children*, London: Routledge.

Cooper, P., Drummond, M. J., Hart, S., Lovey, J. and McLaughlin, C. (2000) *Positive Alternatives to Exclusion*, London: RoutledgeFalmer.

Crozier, J. and Anstiss, J. (1995) 'Out of the spotlight: girls' experience of disruption', in M. Lloyd-Smith and J. Dwyfor Davies (eds) *On the Margins: the educational experiences of 'problem' pupils*, pp. 31–47, Stoke: Trentham.

Crozier, W. and Dimmock, P. (1999) 'Name-calling and nicknames in a sample of primary school children', *British Journal of Educational Psychology*, 69: 505–16.

Cunningham, J. (1991) 'The human rights secondary school', in H. Starkey (ed.) *The Challenge of Human Rights Education*, pp. 90–104, London: Cassell.

—— (2000) 'Democratic practice in a secondary school', in A. Osler (ed.) *Citizenship and Democracy in Schools: diversity, identity, equality*, Stoke: Trentham.

Daniels, H., Hey, V., Leonard, D. and Smith, M. (1999) 'Issues of equity in special needs education from a gendered perspective', *British Journal of Special Education*, 26 (4): 189–95.

Darlow, N. (2001) *There Must be Something I Can Do*, Wellington: Wellington Community Law Centre.

Davies, L. (1998) *School Councils and Pupil Exclusion*, London: School Councils UK.

Davies, L. and Kirkpatrick, G. (2000) *The Eurodem Project: a review of pupil democracy in Europe*, London: Children's Rights Alliance.

Delamont, S. (1999) 'Gender and the discourse of derision', *Research Papers in Education*, 14 (1): 3–21.

Dennison, C. and Coleman, J. (2000) *Young People and Gender: a review of research*, Report to the Women's Unit, Cabinet Office and Family Policy Unit, Home Office.

Department for Education and Employment (1997) *Permanent Exclusions from Schools in England 1995–96*, London: DfEE.

—— (1999a) *Social Inclusion: pupil support*, Circular 10/99, London: DfEE.

—— (1999b) *Social Inclusion: the LEA role in pupil support*, Circular 19/99, London: DfEE.

—— (1999c) *Tackling Truancy Together: a strategy document*, London: DfEE.

—— (2000) *Guidance on the Education of Children and Young People in Public Care*, London: DfEE.

Department for Education and Skills (2001a) *National Statistics: first release. GCSE/GNVQ and GCE A/AS/VCE/ Advanced GNVQ Results for Young People in England, 2000/01*. SFR 45/20901, 20 November, London: DfES. www.dfes.gov.uk/statistics

—— (2001b) *National Statistics Bulletin. Statistics of Education: permanent exclusions from maintained schools in England*, Issue 10/01, November, London: DfES.

—— (2001c) *Schools Achieving Success: White Paper*, London: The Stationery Office.

—— (2001d) *Pupil Absence and Truancy from Schools in England 2000/2001: Statistical Bulletin*, London: DfES.

—— (2002) *Permanent Exclusions from Schools and Exclusion Appeals, England 2000/2001 (Provisional Estimates)*, 23 May, London: DfES.

Eggleston, J., Dunn, D.K. and Anjali, M. (1986) *Education for Some: the educational and vocational experiences of 15–18 year-old members of minority ethnic groups*, Stoke: Trentham.

Elley, W. (1992) *How in the World do Students Read? IEA study of reading literacy*, Hamburg: International Association for the Evaluation of Educational Achievement.

Elton, R.E. (1989) *Discipline in Schools: report of the Committee of Enquiry chaired by Lord Elton*, London: HMSO.

Epstein, D. and Johnson, R. (1998) *Schooling Sexualities*, Buckingham: Open University Press.

Epstein, D., Elwood, J., Hey, V. and Maw, J. (1998) 'Schoolboy frictions: feminism and "failing" boys', in D. Epstein, J. Elwood, V. Hey and J. Maw (eds) *Failing Boys? Issues in gender and achievement*, pp. 3–18, Buckingham: Open University Press.

Essed, P. (1991) *Understanding Everyday Racism: an interdisciplinary theory*, London: Sage.

Figueroa, P. (1991) *Education and the Social Construction of 'Race'*, London: Routledge.

Florian, L. and Rouse, M. (2001) 'Inclusive practice in English secondary schools: lessons learned', *Cambridge Journal of Education*, 31 (3): 399–12.

Frank, J., Tatum, C. and Tucker, S. (1999) *On Small Shoulders: learning from the experiences of former young carers*, London: Children's Society.

Garden, R. (1997) (ed.) *Mathematics and Science Performance in the Middle Primary: Results from New Zealand's participation in the Third International Mathematics and Science Study*, Wellington: Ministry of Education, Research and International Section.

Gerrard, N. (2002) 'Why are so many teenage girls cutting themselves?' *Observer*, 19 May: 16–17.

Gilbert, R. and Gilbert, P. (1998) *Masculinity Goes to School*, Sydney: Allen and Unwin.

Gilbertson, D. (1998) 'Exclusion and crime', in N. Donovan (ed.) *Second Chances: exclusion from school and equality of opportunity*, pp. 24–28, London: New Policy Institute.

Gillborn, D. (1990) *'Race', Ethnicity and Education: teaching and learning in multi-ethnic schools*, London: Hyman.

—— (1998) 'Exclusion from school: an overview of the issues', in N. Donovan (ed.) *Second Chances: exclusion from school and equality of opportunity*, pp. 11–18, London: New Policy Institute.

Gillborn, D. and Mirza, H. S. (2000) *Educational Inequality: mapping race, class and gender – A synthesis of research evidence*, HMI 232, London: OFSTED.

Gillborn, D. and Youdell, D. (2000) *Rationing Education: policy, practice, reform and equity*, Buckingham: Open University Press.

Graham, J. and Bowling, B. (1995) *Young People and Crime*, London: Home Office.

Griffin, C. (1993) *Representations of Youth: the study of youth and adolescence in Britain and America*, Cambridge: Polity Press.

—— (2000) 'Discourses of crisis and loss: analysing the "boys' under-achievement" debate', *Journal of Youth Studies*, 3 (2): 167–88.

Haraway, D. (1991) *Simians, Cyborgs and Women: the reinvention of nature*, London: Free Association Books.

Harris, N. and Eden, K. with Blair, A. (2000) *Challenges to School Exclusion: exclusion, appeals and the law*, London: RoutledgeFalmer.

Hatcher, R. (1998) 'Social justice and the politics of school effectiveness and improvement', *Race Ethnicity and Education*, 1 (2): 267–89.

Hayden, C. (1997) *Children Excluded from Primary School: debates, evidence, responses*, Buckingham: Open University Press.

Hayes, D. (1998) 'The displacement of girls as the "educationally disadvan-taged" subject: a genealogical tale', *Change: Transformations in Education* 1 (2): 7–15.

Hey, V. (1997) *The Company She Keeps: an ethnography of girls' friendship*, Buckingham: Open University Press.

Hey, V., Leonard, D., Daniels, H. and Smith, M. (1998) 'Boys' under-achievement, special needs practices and questions of equity', in D. Epstein, J. Elwood, V. Hey and J. Maw, (eds) *Failing Boys? Issues in gender and achievement*, 128–44, Buckingham: Open University Press.

Hill, A. and Helmore, E. (2002) 'Mean Girls', *Observer*, 3 March: 19.

Hinds, D. (2002) 'Girl trouble: the hidden problem', *Independent*, 14 February: 6.

House of Commons (1998) *Select Committee on Education and Employment Fifth Report: tackling disaffection*, London: House of Commons.

Howe, C. (1997) *Gender and Classroom Interaction: a research review*, Edinburgh: Scottish Council for Research in Education.

Jackson, D. (1998) 'Breaking out of the binary trap: boys' underachieve-ment, schooling and gender relations', in D. Epstein. J. Elwood. V. Hey and J. Maw, (eds) *Failing Boys? Issues in gender and achievement*, 77–95, Buckingham: Open University Press.

Jasper, L. (2002) 'Macpherson: was it all a waste of time?' Edited version of lecture delivered on 20 February 2002, *Royal Society of Arts Journal*, 2 (6): 30–32.

Jeffs, T. (2002) 'Schooling, education and children's rights', in B. Franklin (ed.) *The New Handbook of Children's Rights: comparative policy and practice*, pp. 45–59, London: RoutledgeFalmer.

Johnson, C. (2002) 'Don't just say yes to exclusion', *Times Educational Supplement*, 5 July: 31.

Keenan, K., Loeber, R. and Green, S. (1999) 'Conduct disorder in girls: a review of the literature', *Clinical Child and Family Psychology Review*, 2 (1): 3–19.

Kelly, A. (1988) 'Gender differences in teacher–pupil interactions: a meta-analytic review', *Research in Education*, 39, 1–23.

Kenway, J. and Kelly, P. (2000) 'Local global labour markets and the restructuring of gender, schooling and work, in N. Stromquist and K. Monkman (eds), *Globalisation and Education: integration and contestation across cultures*, Lanham, MD: Rowman and Littlefield.

Kenway, J. and Willis, S. with Blackmore, J. and Rennie. L (1998) *Answering Back: girls, boys and feminism in schools*, London: Routledge.

Kochhar, C. A. (1997) 'The role of aid agencies and academic institutions in reducing educational dependence', in J. Lynch, C. Modgil and S. Modgil (eds) *Education and Development: tradition and innovation. Volume 1: Concepts, approaches and assumptions*, pp. 104–132, London: Cassell.

Kraack, A. and Kenway J. (2002) 'Place, time and stigmatised youthful identities: bad boys in paradise', *Journal of Rural Sociology*, 18(2): 145–55.

Lansdown, G. and Newell, P. (1994) *UK Agenda for Children*, London: Children's Rights Development Unit.

Lloyd, G. (2000) 'Gender and exclusion from school', in J. Salisbury and S. Riddell (eds) *Gender, Policy and Educational Change*, pp. 257–72, London: Routledge.

Lloyd, G. and O'Regan, A. (1999) 'Education for social exclusion? Issues to do with the effectiveness of educational provision for young women with "social, emotional and behavioural difficulties"', *Emotional and Behavioural Difficulties*, 4 (2): 38–46.

—— (2000) '"You have to learn to love yourself cos no one else will". Young women with "social, emotional or behavioural difficulties" and the idea of the underclass', *Gender and Education*, 12 (1): 39–52.

Lloyd, G., Stead, J. and Kendrick, A. (2001) *Hanging On In There: a study of inter-agency work to prevent school exclusion in three local authorities*, London: National Children's Bureau.

Loxley, A. and Thomas, G. (2001) 'Neo-conservatives, neo-liberals, the New Left and inclusion: stirring the pot', *Cambridge Journal of Education*, 31 (3): 291–301.

Lynch, J. (1997) 'Introduction: the purpose, context and structure of the series', in: J. Lynch, C. Modgil and S. Modgil (eds) *Education and Development: tradition and innovation. Volume 1: Concepts, approaches and assumptions*, pp. ix–xxv, London: Cassell.

Mac an Ghaill, M. (1994) *The Making of Men: masculinities, sexualities and schooling*, Buckingham: Open University Press.

—— (1996) '"What about the boys?" Schooling, class and crisis masculinity', *Sociological Review*, 44 (3): 381–97.

Macpherson, W. (1999) *The Stephen Lawrence Inquiry*, London: The Stationery Office.

Macrae, S. and Maguire, M. (2000) 'All change, no change. Gendered regimes in the post-sixteen setting', in J. Salisbury and S. Riddell (eds) *Gender, Policy and Educational Change*, pp. 169–87, London: Routledge.

Mann, C. (1998) 'The impact of working-class mothers on the educational success of their adolescent daughters at a time of social change', *British Journal of Sociology of Education*, 19 (2): 211–26.

Massey, D. (1993) ' "Power-geometry" and a progressive sense of place', in J. Bird, B. Curtis, G. Robertson and L. Tricker (eds) *Mapping the Futures: local culture, global change*, Routledge: London.

Meltzer, H., Harrington, R., Goodman, R. and Jenkins, R. (2001) *Children and Adolescents Who Try to Harm, Hurt or Kill Themselves*, London: Office for National Statistics.

Mills, M. (2001) *Challenging Violence in Schools: an issue of masculinities*, Buckingham: Open University Press.

Ministry of Education (2001) *A Report on Stand-downs, Suspensions, Exclusions and Expulsions*, April, Wellington, New Zealand: Ministry of Education.

Mirza, H.S. (1992) *Young, Female and Black*, London: Routledge.

Munn, P., Lloyd, G. and Cullen, M. A. (2000) *Alternatives to Exclusion from School*, London: Paul Chapman.

Murphy, P. and Elwood, J. (1998) 'Gendered learning outside and inside school: influences on achievement', in D. Epstein, J. Elwood, V. Hey and J. Maw (eds) *Failing Boys? Issues in gender and achievement*, pp. 162–181, Buckingham: Open University Press.

Newell, P. (1991) *The UN Convention and Children's Rights in the UK*, London: National Children's Bureau.

Office for Standards in Education (1996) *Exclusions from Secondary Schools 1995/6*, London: OFSTED.

—— (2001) *Improving Attendance and Behaviour in Secondary Schools: strategies to promote educational inclusion*, London: The Stationery Office.

Office for Standards in Education and Equal Opportunities Commission (1996) *The Gender Divide: performance differences between boys and girls at school*, London: HMSO (Equal Opportunities Commission).

Osborn, M. (1999) 'National context, educational goals and pupil experience of schooling and learning in three European countries', *Compare*, 29 (3): 287–301.

Osler, A. (1989) *Speaking Out: black girls in Britain*, London: Virago.

—— (1994) 'Still hidden from history? The representation of women in recently published history textbooks', *Oxford Review of Education*, 20 (2): 219–35.

—— (1997a) *Exclusion from School and Racial Equality (Research Report)*, London: Commission for Racial Equality.

—— (1997b) 'Teachers' biographies and educational development', *International Journal of Educational Development*, 17 (4): 361–71.

—— (1997c) *The Education and Careers of Black Teachers: changing identities, changing lives*, Buckingham: Open University Press.

—— (1999a) 'The educational experiences and career aspirations of black and ethnic minority undergraduates', *Race, Ethnicity and Education*, 2 (1): 39–58.

—— (1999b) 'Citizenship, democracy and political literacy', *Multicultural Teaching*, 18 (1): 12–15 & 29.

—— (2000) 'Children's rights, responsibilities and understandings of school discipline', *Research Papers Education*, 15 (1): 49–67.

—— (2002) 'Citizenship education and the strengthening of democracy: is race on the agenda?' in D. Scott and H. Lawson (eds) *Citizenship, Education and the Curriculum*, pp. 63–80, Westport: Greenwood.

Osler, A. and Hill, J. (1999) 'Exclusion from school and racial equality: an examination of government proposals in the light of recent research evidence', *Cambridge Journal of Education*, 29 (1): 33–62.

Osler, A. and Hussain, Z. (1995) 'Parental choice and schooling: some factors influencing Muslim mothers' decisions about the education of their daughters', *Cambridge Journal of Education*, 25 (3): 327–47.

Osler, A. and Morrison, M. (2000) *Inspecting Schools for Race Equality: OFSTED's strengths and weaknesses*, Stoke: Trentham, for the Commission for Racial Equality.

—— (2002) 'Can race equality be inspected? Challenges for policy and practice raised by the OFSTED school inspection framework', *British Educational Research Journal*, 28 (3): 327–38.

Osler, A. and Osler, C. (2002) 'Inclusion, exclusion and children's rights: a case study of a student with Asperger syndrome', *Emotional and Behavioural Difficulties*, 7 (1): 35–54.

Osler, A. and Starkey, H. (1996) *Teacher Education and Human Rights*, London: David Fulton.

—— (1998) 'Children's rights and citizenship: some implications for the management of schools', *International Journal of Children's Rights*, 6, 313–33.

—— (2000a) 'Citizenship, human rights and cultural diversity', in A. Osler (ed.) *Citizenship and Democracy in Schools: diversity, identity, equality*, pp. 3–17, Stoke: Trentham.

—— (2000b) 'Human rights, responsibilities and school self-evaluation', in A. Osler (ed.) *Citizenship and Democracy in Schools: diversity, identity, equality*, pp. 91–109, Stoke: Trentham.

—— (2001a) 'Legal perspectives on values, culture and education: human rights, responsibilities and values in education', in J. Cairns, D. Lawton and R. Gardner (eds) *Values, Culture and Education. World Yearbook of Education 2001*, pp. 85–103, London: Kogan Page.

—— (2001b) 'Young people in Leicester (UK): community, identity and citizenship', *Interdiologos*, 2 (1): 48–49.

—— (2002a) 'Education for citizenship: mainstreaming the fight against racism?' *European Journal of Education*, 37 (2): 143–59.

—— (2002b) 'Learning to live together: young people as cosmopolitan citizens', in F. Audigier and N. Bottani (eds), *Education et vivre ensemble. Actes du colloque 'La problematique du vivre ensemble et les curricula' (Learning to live together and curricular contents)*, pp. 133–44, Geneva: SRED.

Osler, A. and Vincent, K. (2002) *Citizenship and the Challenge of Global Education*, Stoke: Trentham.

Osler, A., Watling, R. and Busher, H. (2000) *Reasons for Exclusion from School*, London: Department for Education and Employment.

Osler, A., Street, C., Lall, M. and Vincent, K. (2002) *Not a Problem? Girls and school exclusion*, London: National Children's Bureau.

Paechter, C. (1998) *Educating the Other: gender, power and schooling*, London: Falmer Press.

Parekh, B. (2000) *The Future of Multi-Ethnic Britain. Report of the Commission on the Future of Multi-Ethnic Britain*, London: Profile Books.

Parker-Jenkins, M., Hartas, D., Irving, B. and Barker, V. (1999) *Inclusion, Exclusion and Cultural Awareness: career services supporting the career aspirations of Muslim girls*, Paper presented at the European Conference on Educational Research, Lahti, Finland, 22–25 September.

Parsons, C. (1999) *Education, Exclusion and Citizenship*, London: Routledge.

Parsons, C. and Howlett, K. (1995) 'Difficult dilemmas', *Education*, pp. 22–29, December.

Phoenix, A. (1991) *Young Mothers*, Cambridge: Polity Press.

Plummer, G. (2000) *Failing Working Class Girls*, Stoke: Trentham.

Pomeroy, E. (2000) *Experiencing Exclusion*, Stoke: Trentham.

Rae, C. (2001) *Talking to Young Parents. Teenage parents in North Braunstone*, Leicester: Turning Point Women's Centre.

Reay, D. (2001) ' "Spice Girls", "Nice Girls", "Girlies", and "Tomboys": gender discourses, girls' cultures and femininities in the primary classroom', *Gender and Education*, 13 (2): 153–66.

Reid, K. (1999) *Truancy and Schools*, London: Routledge.

Roker, D., Player, K. and Coleman, J. (1999) 'Young people's voluntary and campaigning activities as sources of political education', *Oxford Review of Education*, 25 (1 & 2): 185–98.

Ruddock, J., Chaplain, R. and Wallace, G. (1996) *School Improvement: what can pupils tell us?* London: David Fulton.

Salisbury, J. and Jackson, D. (1996) *Challenging Macho Values: practical ways of working with adolescent boys*, London: Falmer.

Schools Health Education Unit (2000) *Young People in 1999*, Schools Health Education Unit, University of Exeter.

Seager, J. (1997) *The State of Women in the World Atlas*, London: Penguin.

Sewell, T. (1997) *Black Masculinities and Schooling: how Black boys survive modern schooling*, Stoke: Trentham.

—— (2001) 'Behaviour, race and inclusion: getting inside the black child and not finding Darwin', *Emotional and Behavioural Difficulties*, 6 (3): 167–85.

Social Exclusion Unit (1998) *Truancy and School Exclusion*, London: Cabinet Office.
——— (1999) *Teenage Pregnancy*, London: Cabinet Office.
Spender, D. and Sarah, E. (1980) (eds) *Learning to Lose: sexism and education*, London: The Women's Press.
Standing Committee of Education and Training (2002), Report of the Inquiry into the Education of Boys. Boys: Getting it right, http://www.aph.gov.au/house/committee/edt/Eofb/index.HTM
Stanley, L. and Arora, T. (1998) 'Social exclusion amongst adolescent girls: their self-esteem and coping strategies', *Educational Psychology in Practice*, 14 (2): 94–100.
Stromquist, N. (1998) 'Agents in women's education: some trends in the African context', in M. Bloch, J. A. Beoku-Betts and B. R. Tabachnick (eds) *Women and Education in Sub-Saharan Africa: power, opportunities and constraints*, pp. 25–46, Boulder, Colorado: Lynne Rienner.
Sutton, J. (2001) 'Bullies: thugs or thinkers?' *The Psychologist*, 14 (10): 530–34.
Thacker, J., Strudwick, D. and Babbedge, E. (2002) *Educating Children with Emotional and Behavioural Difficulties: inclusive practice in mainstream schools*, London: RoutledgeFalmer.
Thorne, S. (1996) 'Children's rights and the listening school: an approach to counter bullying among primary school pupils', in A. Osler, H-F. Rathenow and H. Starkey (eds) *Teaching for Citizenship in Europe*, pp. 169–80, Stoke: Trentham.
Tikly, L., Osler, A., Hill, J. and Vincent, K. (2002) *Ethnic Minority Achievement Grant: analysis of LEA action plans*, London, Department for Education and Skills.
Tisdall, G. and Dawson, R. (1994) 'Listening to children: interviews with children attending a mainstream support facility', *Support for Learning*, 9 (4): 179–83.
Troyna, B. (1984) 'Fact or artefact? The "educational underachievement" of black pupils', *British Journal of Sociology of Education*, 5 (2): 153–60.
Troyna, B. and Hatcher, R. (1992) *Racism in Children's Lives*, London: Routledge.
United Nations (1995) *Human Development Report 1995*, Oxford: Oxford University Press.
United Nations Educational Scientific and Cultural Organisation (1995a) *Declaration and Integrated Framework of Action on Education for Peace, Human Rights and Democracy*, Paris: UNESCO.
——— (1995b) *UNESCO Statistical Yearbook 1995*, Paris: UNESCO.
Verhellen, E. (2000) 'Children's rights and education', in A. Osler (ed.) *Citizenship and Democracy in Schools: diversity, identity, equality*, pp. 33–43, Stoke: Trentham.
Vincent, K. and Ballard, K. (1997) 'Living on the margins: lesbian

experiences in secondary schools', *New Zealand Journal of Educational Studies*, 32 (2): 147–61.

Wagemaker, H. (1993) *Achievements in Reading Literacy: New Zealand's performance in a national and international context*, Wellington: Ministry of Education, Research Section.

Walkerdine, V., Lucey, H. and Melody, J. (2001) *Growing Up Girl: psychosocial explorations of gender and class*, Basingstoke: Macmillan-Palgrave.

Weiner, G. (1985) *Just a Bunch of Girls: feminist approaches to schooling*, Milton Keynes: Open University Press.

West, P. (1995) *Giving Boys a Ray of Hope: masculinity and education*, Sydney: Discussion Paper for the Gender Equity Taskforce, Australia.

Whitehead, S. and Barrett, F. (2001) *The Masculinities Reader*, Cambridge: Polity Press.

Whitelaw, S., Milosevic, L. and Daniels, S. (2000) 'Gender, behaviour and achievement: a preliminary study of pupil perceptions and attitudes', *Gender and Education*, 12 (1): 87–113.

Williams, E. (2002) 'Girls who give up', *Times Educational Supplement*, 4 January: 22.

Wilson, A. (1978) *Finding a Voice: Asian women in Britain*, London: Virago.

Wragg, E. (1997) 'Oh Boy', *Times Educational Supplement*, p. 24, 16 May.

Wright, C. (1992) *Race Relations in the Primary School*, London: David Fulton.

Wright, C., Weekes, D. and McGlaughlin, A. (2000) *Race, Class and Gender in Exclusion from School*, London: Falmer.

Wynn, J. and White, J. (1997) *Rethinking Youth*, London: Sage.

Index